Grand Junction

Hiking Guide

Grand Junction Hiking Guide

Steve Kolarik

WestWinds Press®

P R U E T T
THE PRUETT SERIES

Library of Congress Cataloging-in-Publication Data
Kolarik, Steve, 1962-
Grand Junction hiking guide / Steve Kolarik.
    p. cm.
Includes index.
ISBN 0-87108-925-4
    1. Hiking--Colorado--Grand Junction Region--Guidebooks.
    2. Trails--Colorado--Grand Junction Region--Guidebooks.
    3. Grand Junction
Region (Colo.)--Guidebooks. I. Title.
    GV199.42.C6K65 2001
    796.52'09788'17--dc21

                                        2003008691

WestWinds Press®
An imprint of Graphic Arts Books
P.O. Box 56118
Portland, OR 97238-6118
(503) 254-5591
www.graphicartsbooks.com

Designed by Dave Consulting & Hungry Dog Studios
Cover Photo by Eric Wunrow/Maps by Michael Dyer

Table of Contents

Preface

When I started to write this guidebook, I immediately became overwhelmed by conflict. I wanted to share with others the hidden treasures of the Grand Junction area, but I was concerned that the book would contribute to the deterioration of land that popularity can bring.

Eventually, I decided to write this guide book on one premise: It takes as many people to save an area as it does to destroy it. I hope and pray that the people who purchase this guidebook will be enlightened by the tremendous aesthetic value of the Grand Junction area. I hope and pray that people will not only love this land but also be inspired to step forward and actively participate in preserving it as wildlife habitat.

Let's go hiking.

About the Author

Steve is an experienced Colorado Outward Bound instructor and mountain guide. A well-traveled schoolteacher, Steve has taught students in remote regions of the Navajo Indian Reservation as well as along the Mexican Border in Southern Arizona. Presently, Steve works as a special education teacher in Grand Junction where he instructs alternative middle school students.

Introduction

In my travels, I frequently meet people who claim they have driven through Grand Junction, stopped for gas and a burger, and then continued along their way without giving Grand Junction much thought. If travelers only knew—only knew those salmon-colored cliffs to the south host outstanding canyons equal in beauty and splendor to the Canyonlands of Utah. If travelers only knew that those washed-out cliffs to the northwest offer excellent hiking in a solitude setting through one of only three wild horse preserves in the United States. If travelers only knew that the big uprise to the southeast is the world's largest flat-topped mountain. If they only knew ...

Once called "Grand Junkyard" by professional football coach and commentator John Madden, Grand Junction has transformed from a justly called junkyard into a progressive community that is quickly becoming known for its recreational activities and its high-quality lifestyle. This one-time oil shale bust town is now known as Colorado's wine country and is a nationally acclaimed mountain biking destination, and soon to be recognized for its world class hiking.

Located at 4,600 feet elevation, Grand Junction is a pure desert environment hosting the junction of two major rivers, the Gunnison River and the Colorado River. Rainfall is minimal, averaging only between eight and nine inches per year. Winters are mild. Residents may see snow, but never find a need to shovel; instead, they allow the sun to do their work.

Grand Junction was one of the last valleys of the West to be inhabited by pioneer Americans. The first of inhabitants, the Fremont Indians, gave way to the Ute Indians who were guided by the famous Chief Ouray. The Spanish also left their influence in the Grand Valley traveling through looking for gold and passage to California.

Today, Grand Junction and the Grand Valley are a burgeoning community with a population of over 100,000 people. The mild climate and multiplicity of activities has made the area popular among retired citizens. The valley's major employers are the public schools and medical-related services.

Grand Junction, the passer-through community, once called Grand Junkyard, is no more. Come see for yourself.

MOUNTAIN BIKING

The Grand Valley, in addition to hosting marvelous hiking trails, has world class mountain biking trails. This guide has listed only a few trails that are shared with bicycles. Efforts were made to keep this book purely a hikers' guide. There are, however, some nonlisted mountain bike trails that are well worth hiking. One example would be the "Mary's Loop," located near Fruita.

In an ethical pitch to hikers and mountain bikers, I think it is important to remember that the foes of wildland preservation are many. Mountain bikers and hikers are much more alike than different. It is unproductive for these two groups to quarrel over minor differences. Instead, let mountain bikers and hikers embrace their common interests and strengthen in unity to preserve and defend the beautiful wildlands we love and cherish.

DINOSAURS

Rich in dinosaur history, Grand Junction has become part of the Dinosaur Diamond. The Dinosaur Diamond encompasses areas in western Colorado and eastern Utah that are rich in dinosaur fossils. In addition, Fruita has an excellent dinosaur museum that features attractions for children as well as adults. A marvelous hike to observe dinosaur fossils in their natural setting is the Trail Through Time, located in Rabbit Valley. For further information on dinosaurs, contact the Fruita Visitor Center (970-858-8486), 552 Jurassic Ct., Fruita, CO 81521.

NONHIKING ACTIVITIES

Grand Junction offers numerous side attractions to hiking. As previously mentioned, Grand Junction has world-class mountain biking trails. A road bike ride through the Colorado National

Monument is breathtaking in more ways than one. The dinosaur museum is not to be missed, especially if you have children. My favorite nonhiking activity, however, is wine tasting. The Grand Valley produces wines that stack up to the very best California has to offer. You will need to go to Palisade for wine country; and once in Palisade, you can make a loop through Palisade and East Orchard Mesa, hitting several excellent wineries. Unlike those in California, the wineries are seldom crowded, and sample tastings are unlimited. Other Grand Junction attractions include raft trips through Ruby and Horsethief Canyon of the Colorado River, various festivals—including the peach and wine festivals—buying locally grown fruits and vegetables from the numerous farmers' markets, and last, visiting our beautiful downtown shopping area, which displays numerous sculptures and other fine works of art. For further information on Grand Junction's attractions, contact the Grand Junction Visitor Center (970-244-1480), located at the intersection of I-70 and Horizon Drive.

FOOD

Culinary choices in Grand Junction are abundant. Listed below are some of my favorite restaurants:

All American—Old Chicago's, 120 North Ave., 970-244-8383
Breakfast—The Crystal Café & Bake Shop, 314 Main Street, 970-242-8843
Italian—Il Bistro Italiano, 400 Main St., 970-243-8622
Japanese & Sushi—Suehiro Japanese Restaurant, 541 Main St., 970-245-9548
Mexican—Fiesta Guadalajara, 710 North Ave., 970-255-6609
Micro-Brew—Rockslide Brew Pub, 401 Main St., 970-245-2111
New World—Chefs, 936 North Ave., 970-243-9673
Pizza—Pablo's Pizza, 319 Main Street, 970-255-8879
Thai—Ying Thai Restaurant, 757 U.S. Highway 50, 970-245-4866

How To Use This Guide

GETTING HERE

Grand Junction is located in the center of the western region of Colorado. East/west travelers will use Interstate 70; north/south travelers will use Highway 50. Grand Junction has a regional airport offering direct service to Denver, Phoenix, and Salt Lake City. Driving distance between Grand Junction and Denver is 246 miles; between Salt Lake and Grand Junction, 285 miles; and between Phoenix and Grand Junction, 572 miles.

BEST TIME OF YEAR TO TRAVEL

Hiking is a year round activity in Grand Junction. Summers are hot in the desert and require early morning or evening starts. Otherwise, hikers are wise to hike in the higher elevations of the Grand Mesa and Uncompahgre Plateau. Winters are off limits for hiking in the high country, but the desert is inviting. Spring and fall typically bring ideal temperatures for hiking in the desert lands.

CAMPING & ACCOMMODATIONS

Grand Junction has an array of hotel accommodations that will meet the needs of budget as well as first-class travelers. Camping on BLM lands and Forest Service lands for the most part is free, unless otherwise posted. The Devils Canyon area is one place, for example, that does not allow camping. Pay camping is available at any number of campgrounds in the Grand Valley. The Grand Mesa offers Forest Service "fee area" camping, and the Uncompahgre Plateau has numerous opportunities for free camping in choice sites. Forest Service and BLM campgrounds do not offer showers. The easiest place to camp free of charge in the Grand Valley is at the base of the Book Cliffs on BLM lands. Perhaps the most scenic camping location in the area is the campground in the Colorado National Monument; although it is difficult to secure a site at times, it's well worth the try. Another choice camping area that offers showers is Highline Lake State Park (see Highline Lake State Park in trail descriptions).

RECOMMENDED HIKES

Recommending hikes is a terribly subjective affair. However, due to the large number of hikes available in this guide, I felt it necessary to offer some guidance on this matter. I have devised a three-star system: After the title of each hike listed, readers will find one, two, three, or no stars. Three stars represent the finest-quality hike; two stars, a lesser degree than the finest; one star a still lesser degree; and no stars, even less. Remember, take this rating system with a grain of salt. You may absolutely love a hike that I have given no stars.

ACCESS & STARTING POINTS

Although the auto industry may lead you to believe you need a SUV to experience the great outdoors, in Grand Junction the truth is you just don't need it. I drive an old two-wheel drive van with fair ground clearance. The van had no problem getting me to all the trailheads.

The beginning of all route descriptions start at the Grand Junction Visitor Center. The center is located at the intersection of Interstate 70 and Horizon Drive. The visitor center can be reached by telephone at 970-244-1480.

Included in the trail descriptions are maps that should provide you with adequate guidance. If more finely detailed maps are desired, one may obtained them at any local outdoor shop or at the BLM office located at 2815 H Road (close to the visitor center and airport).

GEOLOGY

The geology of the Grand Junction area is a virtual smorgasbord. The western region of the area is part of the Colorado Plateau. Hikers will experience classic deep red sandstone canyons reminiscent to those found in the Canyonlands of Utah. Rattlesnake Canyon for example, boasts one of the largest concentration of arches in the world. Traveling through Unaweep Canyon, one will experience 800 feet of vertical granite rock faces; these were formed by the same forces that sculptured Yosemite Valley in California. The Grand Mesa, in addition to having numerous natural lakes, is the world's largest flat-top mountain.

The Book Cliffs, which create the northern skyline of the valley, is a long narrow vertical sandstone uprise that stretches well over 200 miles to the west. Further knowledge of Grand Junction geology is best gained through other published sources readily available at local bookstores.

FIVE DIFFERENT LAND MANAGERS

There are four major governing bodies responsible for overseeing Grand Junction public lands. The Colorado National Monument is governed by the National Park Service. Be prepared to pay a fee upon entering the monument. The Forest Service governs most of the Uncompahgre Plateau and the Grand Mesa. All city trails are managed by the city of Grand Junction, Highline and Connected Lakes State Parks are managed by Colorado State Parks, and many other lands are managed by the Bureau of Land Management (BLM).

WILDERNESS

In 2001, through diligent efforts by local and nonlocal activists, the Black Ridge Wilderness Study Area officially became wilderness and is now part of the Colorado Canyons National Conservation Area. Efforts like this are absolutely vital for the long-term protection of our nation's wildlands. The plants and animals of our wildlands cannot speak on their own behalf. We must be their voices. Grand Junction has several Wilderness Study Areas that, with sufficient support, may be protected as wilderness. I call out to all people to become involved in local and national issues concerning the protection of our wildlands. There are numerous environmental agencies to choose from. Grand Junction local activists may wish to affiliate with:

Western Colorado Congress - 970-256-7650
P.O. Box 1931, Grand Junction, CO 81502

Colorado Environmental Coalition - 970-243-0002
1000 N. 9th #29, Grand Junction CO 81501

Colorado Mountain Club - 303-279-3080
710 10th Street, Suite 200, Golden, CO 80401

The Sierra Club - 970-242-4862
P.O. Box 1543, Grand Junction, CO 81502

Grand Valley Audubon Society - 970-241-4670
P.O. Box 1211, Grand Junction, CO 81502

Each of these agencies has a slightly different mission statement, so feel them out to find a suitable match. But, by all means, please do get involved!

OFF-ROAD VEHICLES

Off-road vehicles have caused catastrophic damage to our wildlands. Land destroyed by a tire track can take years to regenerate. Once a person has driven off road, other drivers, poorly informed, mistakenly take the tracks as a road. The next thing you know, you've got an illegally-created eyesore that has destroyed habitat for plants and animals. Drivers, please be responsible with your vehicles!

CRYPTOBIOTIC CRUST

Cryptogamic soil is a unique feature to the deserts of the Colorado Plateau. It is a dark brown organism that looks like a miniature cityscape. Cryptobiotic crust grows on barren land and is a critical soil stabilizer. The crust prevents erosion, retains water, and supplies necessary nitrogen for future plant communities. Cryptogams, which may take a century to mature, can be destroyed by a few footprints. Staying on established trails or walking in washes will help you avoid walking through the cryptogams.

POTHOLES AND PLUNGE POOLS

The majority of trails in this guide lay in the desert lands. Desert environments are extremely fragile. It is very important to remember that your impact can seriously affect the health of the environment. Potholes full of water and plunge pools offer vital water for animals. When humans place their hands in potholes, or swim in plunge pools, oils from our bodies (i.e., sun screen, lotions, natural body oils) enter the water and form a fine oil film that floats on top of the water. This fine film makes water undrinkable for wildlife. It is best to carry your own water and leave the potholes and plunge pools to the animals.

PACK IT IN/PACK IT OUT

The message here is very simple: Don't litter! If you had the motivation to carry something into the wildlands, then you should be responsible for carrying that item out of the wildlands.

FIRES

Day hikers have no need for campfires. However, there is the opportunity for multi-day trips in this area. As a person concerned for the preservation of the land, I cannot recommend campfires.

For those of you who insist on a fire, check with local authorities to find out whether there is a ban on campfires in that area. If fires are allowed, please be aware that there are responsible ways to build a fire. First, bring your own firewood rather than deplete a given area of firewood. Second, use preexisting fire pits if possible. When you have finished with your fire, *make sure the fire is out*. Scatter the ring stones and cover/camouflage the fire area so that no one will ever guess a fire was once there. *Never* leave a fire unattended.

ROCK ART

Native American rock art does exist in the Grand Junction area. Please respect the sites by not touching the art. Human oils expelled from hands speed up the erosion process of the unique paintings and carvings. Art found on public lands is best appreciated untouched. Be aware that it is illegal to remove artifacts from public land.

DOGS

Dogs are not allowed on trails in the Colorado National Monument. Dog lovers, do not despair, however. City trails do allow dogs, but they must be on 6-foot leashes. The BLM and Forest Service lands allow dogs to travel unleashed. This statement does not give pet owners the green light to let their dogs run wild, though. Responsible pet owners leash their dogs at populated trailheads. Unleashed dogs should always be under the owner's control; that is, dogs should instantly obey commands from their owners. Pet owners should never allow their dogs to harass wildlife or domestic stock, and they keep their dogs off the cryptogams.

INSECTS

Any hiker who has had a serious bout with gnats will surely agree that it is best to stay away from them at any cost. Gnats are obnoxious flying insects that attack with fury and leave tiny welts on their victims. They are found in the desert lands, and are the thickest near water sources. Gnat season runs from spring to midsummer. The intensity of the season fluctuates from year to year. Some years are thankfully mild, but others are horrific.

Tick season runs about the same time as gnat season. Ticks are more readily found in the scrub oak and pine country of the higher elevations. Large brimmed hats and long-sleeved shirts help protect against ticks. It is always good practice to check your body thoroughly for ticks after your hike.

The Grand Mesa is home to many lakes and billions of mosquitoes. Only a masochist would venture onto the Grand Mesa without insect repellant.

WATER

I cannot emphasize enough that you should carry adequate water when you hike. During the summer months, I carry up to 3 quarts of water on longer hikes. Water acquired from streams, springs, and lakes must always be treated for the parasite called *giardia lamblia*. Iodine tablets picked up at any outdoor shop provide a safe and easy way to decontaminate water. Water filters and pumps work well and produce fresh-tasting water, but it is always possible that they will malfunction. I prefer iodine tablets: They weigh nothing, and they are cheap, easy to use, and guaranteed safe. The only drawback to iodine tablets is that they impart a slight taste of iodine to the water.

HEAT

The deserts of Grand Junction can experience extremely high temperatures during the summer months. Early morning or evening hikes, large brimmed hats, and plenty of water are well advised. It is important to remember that children and elderly people are much more affected by extremely high temperatures.

HYPOTHERMIA

When venturing into particularly higher elevations, hikers should be prepared for unexpected weather changes. Storms move in, winds pick up, you have lost your way, and the sun is going down. For these reasons, always bring extra clothes so that you will stay warm and dry on your hikes. Bringing a lighter so that you can light emergency fires is also a good idea (but remember the safety precautions I have already discussed).

Hypothermia means that your body has lost the battle of keeping itself warm. Death will occur from hypothermia unless an outside heat source is found quickly. Simply placing a hypothermic person into a sleeping bag is not enough; remember, the victim can no longer produce heat. In essence, you are insulating an ice cube. You must crawl into that sleeping bag with the victim to provide him or her a heat source. You may not have the luxury of a sleeping bag on day hikes; however, building a fire and supplying hot drinks are other ways of providing heat to the victim.

LIGHTNING

The number one lightening-prone trail in this guide is the Crag Crest Trail. Early starts to beat the afternoon thunderheads are the best way to avoid lightning. If you are faced with a lightning storm, your safest option is to retreat to a low elevation as quickly as possible.

RELAX, DON'T WORRY

Words of advice for those who are inexperienced regarding the wildlands of the West. Don't worry about wild animals! No, snakes are not hiding behind every rock and waiting to strike at any given opportunity. During all the hiking I have done in this area, I have seen only one rattlesnake. If you are lucky enough to come across a snake or any other wild animal in your travels, just give the animal some room and appreciate it's natural beauty.

The same advice goes for bears and cats. Again, in all my hiking, I have had the opportunity to view only one bear and one bobcat in this area. So please don't hike in fear of animals. They are not out to "get you."

THE DISCLAIMER

The author is in no way responsible for misfortunes hikers may experience from using this guide. It's not my fault if you get lost, benighted, arrested, or eaten. I am, however, concerned about accuracy in this guide. If you stumble across errors in this guide, or feel I have left out worthwhile hikes, please feel free to contact me at: Steve Kolarik, P.O. Box 4192, Grand Junction, CO 81502.

UT   CO

AZ   NM

Area of Detail

Utah
Colorado

Lit

Rabbit
Valley

Highli.
State I

70

Black Ridge
Wilderness

Colorado
National
Monument

To Salt Lake City

70

141

U

Arches
National
Park

Moab

191

46

90

Canyonlands
National
Park

Slick Roc

TN
11.5°

0

U

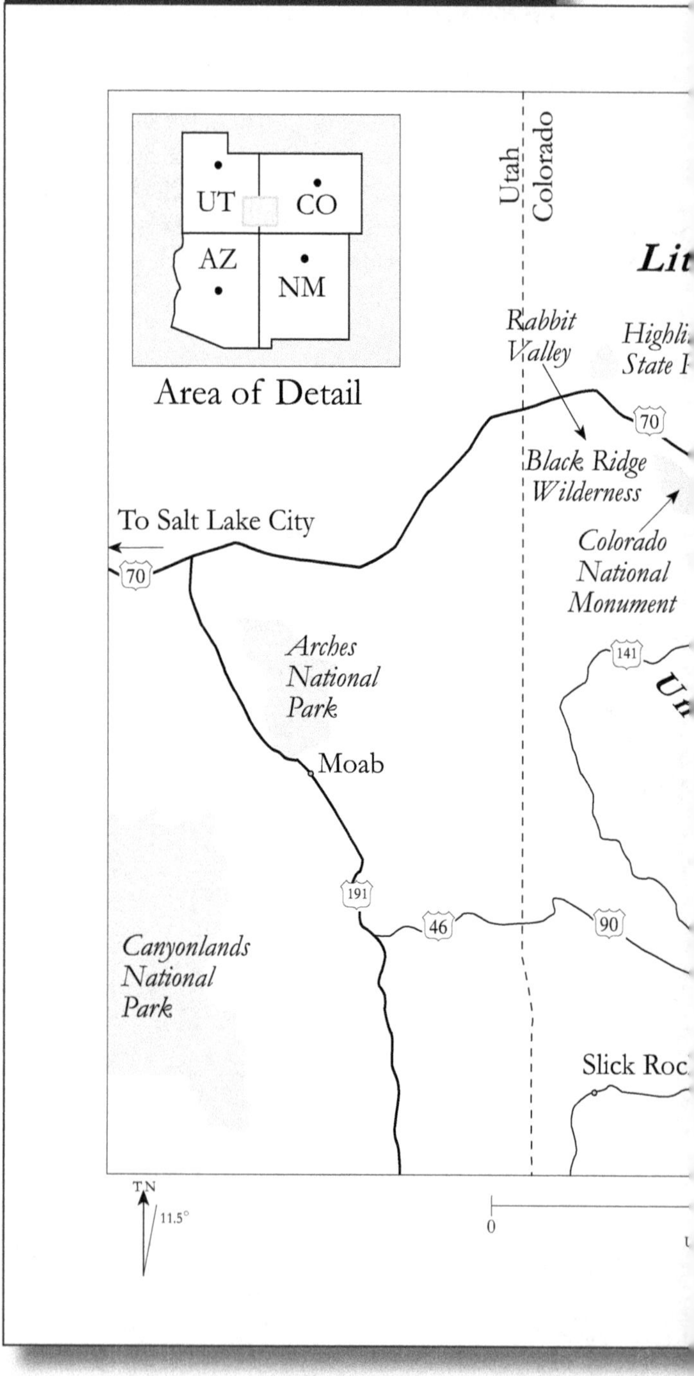

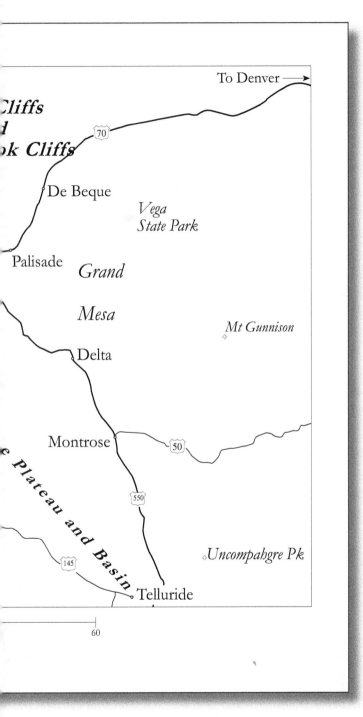

Cliffs
d
ok Cliffs

De Beque

Vega
State Park

Palisade

Grand

Mesa

Delta

Montrose

Uncompahgre Pk

Telluride

To Denver →

Mt Gunnison

70

50

550

145

Plateau and Basin

60

CHAPTER 1

Hiking the Mica Mine Trail

Bangs Canyon Area

The Bangs Canyon area has some wilderness characteristics as well as an "area of critical environmental concern." This means, holy shit, we'd better save this place before the off-road vehicles destroy it! The Tabaguache Trail is a classic mountain-biking trail that cuts through the center of this land and stretches from Grand Junction to Montrose, Colorado.

Bangs Canyon proper is densely vegetated with sage, piñon juniper, and scrub oak. Hikers will spend most of their day following sporadic game trails. Rough Canyon offers a deep narrow canyon; hikers will work their way down the wash by circumnavigating numerous plunge pools. Rough Canyon also has two side canyons, one of them being a short squeeze version of a narrows. Neither of these side canyons should be missed. The Mica Mine Trail is an easy hike along a perennial stream that leads to an abandoned mine still rich with mica deposits. This is a beautiful hike, and it's suitable for the family.

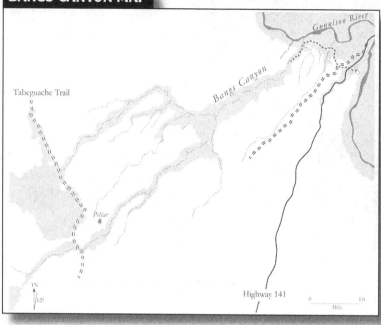

Lower Bangs Canyon

Maps: USGS 7.5 minute maps: Island Mesa, Whitewater
Location: 15 miles from the Grand Junction Visitor Center
Elevation Range: 4,670—5,200 feet
Length of Hike (round trip): Varies. A recommended hike
  (described below) from the mouth of Bangs Canyon to
  the junction of Bangs Canyon and West Bangs Canyon is
  9 miles.
Difficulty Rating: Moderate; some route finding is involved.
Seasons to Hike: Spring, fall, and winter
Special Features: Solitude; wildlife
Services: None
Managing Agency: Bureau of Land Management: Grand Junction
  Resource Area

Access: From the Visitor Center, turn left (southwest) on Horizon
Drive. At the roundabout, continue traveling southwest. Turn
left (south) onto 7th Street, then right onto Ute Avenue and left

(south) onto 5th Street, which eventually turns into Highway 50. Cross the 5th Street Bridge and drive southeast toward Delta on Highway 50. Continue for approximately 8 miles to Whitewater. Travel 0.5 mile to Highway 141 and turn right onto the Unaweep/ Tabeguache Scenic and Historic Byway. Continue for 1.5 miles, crossing a bridge over East Creek. Turn left shortly before reaching a BLM sign and park here.

Trail Description: Cross Highway 141 heading north and look for a walkover fence, where you will pick up the Tabeguache Trail. The Tabeguache Trail is a 142-mile mountain bike trail that runs from Montrose to Grand Junction. Ascend the steep slope of East Creek. Within approximately ten minutes of your hike, you will access a jeep road. Small orange flags mark this site for mountain bike riders. Abandon the trail/road and travel northwest across country. Look for a shallow drainage that runs northwest/ southeast and drop into it. Continue hiking northwest down the drainage for approximately fifteen minutes until you approach a drainage that runs north/south. Travel down (north) the drainage. Within approximately ten minutes, the drainage opens up. Head west at this point to avoid trespassing on the land that borders the Gunnison River. Within roughly fifteen minutes, you will reach the mouth of Bangs Canyon, which is marked by a large grove of cottonwood trees and the Gunnison River. As you hike up the canyon, follow game and cattle trails on the right (north) side of the canyon. Eventually, the vegetation becomes quite thick and large boulders present some obstacles. Trailblazing may be avoided by climbing up the ridge on the left (south) side of the canyon. Hiking from the mouth of the canyon up to the junction with West Bangs Canyon takes approximately two hours. If you are on a day hike, this is a good place to turn back.

Mica Mine Trail **

Maps: USGS 7.5 minute maps: Island Mesa; Glade Park
Location: 11 miles from the Grand Junction Visitor Center
Elevation Range: 6,160—6,200 feet
Length of Hike (round trip): Approximately 1 mile
Difficulty Rating: Easy

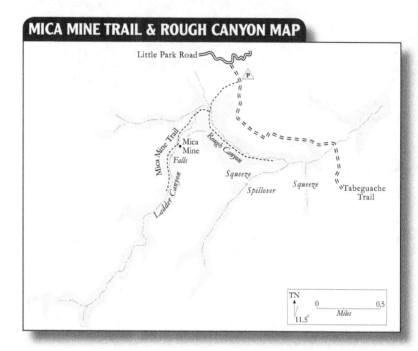

MICA MINE TRAIL & ROUGH CANYON MAP

Little Park Road

P

Mica Mine Trail

Mica Mine

Falls

Rough Canyon

Ladder Canyon

Squeeze

Spillover

Squeeze

Tabeguache Trail

TN

11.5°

0   Miles   0.5

Seasons to Hike: Spring, fall, and winter
Special Features: Interesting geology; year-round creek; scenic
     red sandstone canyon
Services: None
Managing Agency: Bureau of Land Management: Grand Junction
     Resource Area

Access: From the Visitor Center, turn left (southwest) on Horizon
Drive. At the roundabout, continue traveling southwest. Follow
the signs for the Colorado National Monument by turning left
(south) onto 7th Street, and then right (west) onto Grand Avenue.
Pass through a major intersection with Highways 6 and 50 and
cross the Colorado River. Grand Avenue is now Highway 340.
Turn left onto Monument Road. Within 0.25 mile, depart from
the road that leads to the east entrance of the Colorado National
Monument and turn left onto D Road. D Road turns into Rosevale
Road. Within about 1 mile, turn right onto Little Park Road. Take
this road for approximately 5 miles. Watch for a sign indicating
a cattle guard and immediately to your left you will see the BLM
sign for "Bangs Canyon Staging Area." Turn left here and park in
the large staging area on the left (east) side of this gravel road.

Trail Description: From the parking area, cross the dirt road and, heading west, walk down a steep, rough jeep road for a few minutes. Turn right (north) at a trail junction and follow the jeep road. When the jeep road bears left (southwest), watch for a jeep road that climbs out of the canyon on the right. Avoid this and stay low along the creek. Follow the route along the creek as it cuts through the lower portion of Ladder Canyon—another beautiful canyon in the Bangs Canyon Recreation Area. The road ends within thirty minutes of walking. Continue on a trail to the mine. Beyond the mine is a small waterfall. To continue hiking, before you reach the waterfall look for a steep trail on the right side of the creek just beyond a sharp, limestone cliff. Climb the short trail to the rim. Bear left (southwest) and continue up Ladder Canyon for about 2 miles until the trail ends in a large thicket of oak and sagebrush.

Rough Canyon ***

Maps: USGS 7.5 minute map: Island Mesa
Location: 11 miles from the Grand Junction Visitor Center
Elevation Range: 5,520 feet—6,160 feet
Length of Hike (round trip): Varies. A recommended hike
    (described below) is approximately 4 miles.
Difficulty Rating: Moderate
Seasons to Hike: Spring and fall
Special Features: Sheer Wingate sandstone canyon walls; pool
    plunges; slot canyon
Services: None
Managing Agency: Bureau of Land Management: Grand Junction
    Resource Area

Access: From the Visitor Center, turn left (southwest) onto Horizon Drive. At the roundabout, continue traveling southwest. Follow the signs for the Colorado National Monument by turning left (south) onto 7th Street, and then right (west) onto Grand Avenue. Pass through a major intersection with Highways 6 and 50 and cross the Colorado River. Grand Avenue is now Highway 340. Turn left onto Monument Road. Within 0.25 mile, depart from the road that leads to the east entrance of the Colorado National

Monument and turn left onto D Road. This turns into Rosevale Road. Within about 1 mile, turn right onto Little Park Road. Take this road for approximately 5 miles. Watch for a sign indicating a cattle guard and immediately to the left you will see the BLM sign for "Bangs Canyon Staging Area." Turn left here and park in the large staging area on the left (east) side of this gravel road.

Trail Description: From the parking area, cross the dirt road and, heading west, walk down a steep, rough jeep road for a few minutes. Turn left (south) at a trail junction and travel down Rough Canyon. This scenic canyon, flanked by brilliant red sandstone walls, is filled with small pool drops. After about an hour of hiking, look for side canyons on the right (southwest). The first canyon leads hikers to a beautiful spillover. If the water flow is minimal, hikers can scramble up and over the spillover to explore the more distant reaches of this tributary. As you head back down Rough Canyon, look for a second side canyon on the right. This tributary is reached shortly before the canyon opens into a large expanse of slickrock and an impassible drop. Hike up this short canyon to one of the few slot canyons in the area. To explore this short side canyon, work your way up the slot to another spillover. Return to Rough Canyon and pick up a jeep road on the left (north) side of the canyon. This road will lead you back to your vehicle via a long climb on the Kayenta Bench sandstone. Your other option is to head back up Rough Canyon.

Ribbon Trail *

Maps: USGS 7.5 minute map: Grand Junction
Location: 8 miles from the Grand Junction Visitor Center
Elevation Range: 4,800—5,560 feet
Length of Hike (round trip): 2 miles
Difficulty Rating: Although moderate for the most part, the descent into canyon is strenuous.
Seasons to Hike: Spring, fall, and winter
Special Features: Geological formations; canyon views
Services: None
Managing Agency: Bureau of Land Management: Grand Junction Resource Area

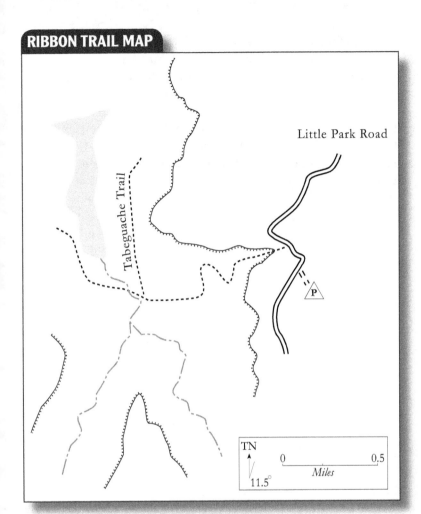

Access: From the Visitor Center, turn left (southwest) onto Horizon Drive. At the roundabout, continue traveling southwest. Follow the signs for the Colorado National Monument by turning left (south) on 7th Street, and then right (west) onto Grand Avenue. Pass through a major intersection with Highways 6 and 50 and cross the Colorado River. Grand Avenue is now Highway 340. Turn left onto Monument Road. Within 0.25 mile, depart from the road that leads to the east entrance of the Colorado National Monument and turn left onto D Road. D Road turns into Rosevale Road. Within about 1 mile, turn right onto Little Park Road. Take this road for approximately 3 miles and park on the left side of the road at the BLM Little Park Staging Area.

Trail Description: Head back down Little Park Road on foot for about a minute until you reach the trailhead on the west side of the road. The trail descends quickly through the rainbow-hued Morrison shale into a drainage. Travel right (west) at this junction down the streambed. Within about five minutes, note the trail on the right that abandons the wash; this is the Tabeguache Trail. Continue hiking down the drainage and look for a trail on the left. Take the trail, which leads you out of the wash and along the south rim of Echo Canyon. The trail now affords an overlook of this box canyon, which can also be accessed from the base of Old Gordon's Trail in the Colorado National Monument. Continue on the trail until it crosses another wash and look for a huge cairn built up around a government survey post. This is a good point to turn back, or you may choose continue up the drainage. Another option is to explore other drainages. From the first junction encountered at the base of the Morrison shale, travel south up the drainage and explore.

CHAPTER 2

Hiking Jones Canyon

Black Ridge Canyons Wilderness Area

The Black Ridge Canyons Wilderness Area, as mentioned earlier, is part of the recently designated Colorado Canyons National Conservation Area—and it's a truly beautiful example of Colorado Plateau wilderness. Solitude, arches, and red sandstone canyons reward hikers who venture here. Rattlesnake Canyon has one of the largest concentration of arches in the world. As impressive as this statement is, I find other canyons of the Black Ridge even more aesthetically pleasing.

Hikers can access the upper regions of the Black Ridge, as well as some of the lower canyon mouths, by vehicle. Accessing the mouths of Mee and Knowles Canyons is best done by taking a trip down the Colorado River. The river route entails a beautiful 30-mile easy flat water trip that passes through the Ruby and Horsethief Canyons of the Colorado River. Embarking on a river

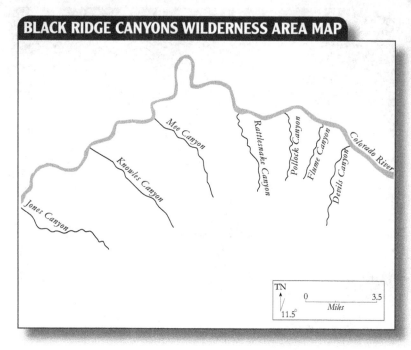

BLACK RIDGE CANYONS WILDERNESS AREA MAP

Mee Canyon

Rattlesnake Canyon

Pollock Canyon

Flume Canyon

Colorado River

Devils Canyon

Knowles Canyon

Jones Canyon

TN
11.5°

0   3,5
        Miles

trip may seem like a great deal of effort to access a canyon; however, the lower Mee and Knowles Canyons are very special places. I have not tested this route; however people claim they have backpacked down Knowles Canyon, traversed the embankments of the Colorado River, and hiked up Mee Canyon.

Devils Canyon ***

Maps: BLM Colorado Canyons National Conservation Area map;
           USGS 7.5 minute maps: Mack, Battleship Rock
Location: 14 miles from the Grand Junction Visitor Center
Elevation Range: 4,600—5,100 feet
Length of Hike (round trip): 6 miles
Difficulty Rating: Moderate
Seasons to Hike: Spring, fall, and winter
Special Features: Scenic sandstone canyon
Services: None
Managing Agency: Bureau of Land Management: Grand Junction
           Resource Area

DEVILS CANYON & FLUME CANYON TRAIL MAP

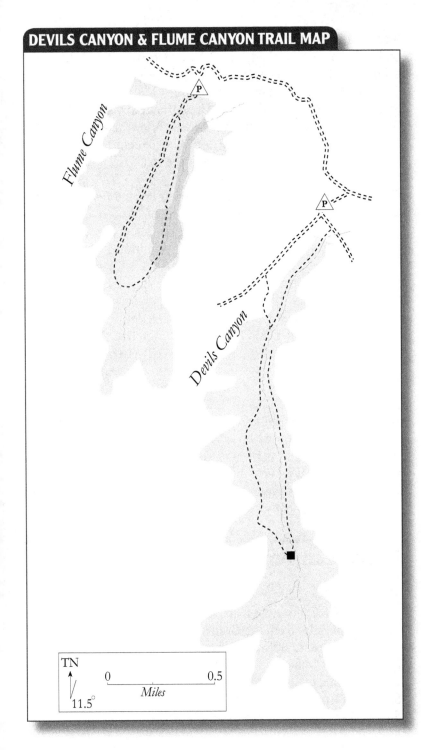

Flume Canyon

Devils Canyon

TN
11.5°

0   0.5
Miles

Access: Drive west on I-70 toward Fruita for approximately 12 miles. Take Exit 19 (Highway 340) and turn left (south) at the stop sign. This road also goes to the west entrance to the Colorado National Monument. Follow the road for 1.3 miles to Kings View Estates. A sign is posted for the Horsethief Canyon Wildlife Area. Turn right (west) onto Kings View Road. After traveling 1.2 miles, bear left when you reach a fork. Continue for about 0.25 mile until you reach the trailhead at the end of the road.

Trail Description: This beautiful canyon is located just west of the Colorado National Monument. Its scenery is spectacular. From the parking area, take the wide path and follow the well-marked signs for Devils Canyon. Within about five minutes, you will come to a fork; either way here will work. Cross the bridge to hike along the streambed. Otherwise, take the right fork and follow a jeep road for about five minutes until you see another fork. Bear left, following the sign for Devils Canyon. When you reach a slickrock wash, look for a cairn and a faint trail to the left. Cross the wash as it leads to the west rim of Devils Creek. The trail continues southwest along the rim as it drops into the canyon. Hike up the canyon for a short distance until you see a BLM Wilderness Area sign. The trail leads up and out of the creek on the right (west) side. The path climbs through the abrupt dark reddish gray rock (Precambrian era) onto a shelf marked by piñon-juniper vegetation. The trail continues to skirt along the sheer canyon walls in a gradual ascent. A good place to stop is at an old cabin located on your left. Note that this area provides habitat to a herd of about 65 desert bighorn sheep.

Flume Canyon

Maps: BLM Colorado Canyons National Conservation Area map; USGS 7.5 minute maps: Mack, Battleship Rock
Location: 16 miles from the Grand Junction Visitor Center
Elevation Range: 4,500—4,800 feet
Length of Hike (round trip): 4.5 miles
Difficulty Rating: Moderate
Seasons to Hike: All seasons
Special Features: Scenic canyon

Services: Restrooms at the Pollack Bench trailhead
Managing Agency: Bureau of Land Management: Grand Junction
Resource Area

Access: Drive west on I-70 toward Fruita for approximately 12 miles. Take Exit 19 (Highway 340) and turn left (south) at the stop sign. This is also the road to take for the west entrance of the Colorado National Monument. Follow the road for about 1 mile to Kings View Estates. A sign is posted for the Horsethief Canyon Wildlife Area. Turn right (west) onto Kings View Road. Within 1 mile, you will bear right at a fork with a sign indicating Devils Canyon. Travel for 2 miles. On the left side of the road, a small BLM trailhead sign is posted by a parking area that will accommodate about three cars. If parking is unavailable, drive on for 0.2 mile to the Pollack Bench trailhead.

Trail Description: From the small parking area, hike along the two-track dirt road. Within a few minutes, you will see to the right a small BLM trail sign pointing to a path that leads to the Pollack Bench Trail. Do not take this. Instead, continue straight on toward a yellow metal gate. Pass through the gate and travel along a wide path through the piñon-juniper forest. Although this trail is a loop, stay on the wide path and travel counterclockwise because it is difficult to find the left fork of the loop. After about 2 miles, the trail becomes a single track and begins its descent into Flume Creek. Once in the creek, travel downstream through the cottonwood trees and red sandstone walls. Eventually, you will reach a huge and impassible drop-off. At this point, the trail continues to run parallel along the west rim of the creek amid splendid views of the sheer-walled canyon. The trail becomes very faint, but eventually it leads to the wide path again and ultimately back to the trailhead.

Jones Canyon Overlook

Maps: BLM Colorado Canyons National Conservation Area map;
USGS 7.5 minute maps: Sieber Canyon, Westwater
Location: 34 miles from the Grand Junction Visitor Center
Elevation Range: 5,600—6,000 feet

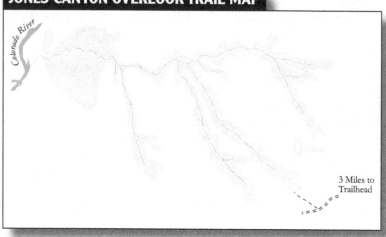

JONES CANYON OVERLOOK TRAIL MAP

3 Miles to
Trailhead

Length of Hike (round trip): 7 miles
Difficulty Rating: Moderate
Seasons to Hike: Spring, summer, and fall
Special Features: Stunning canyon overview; primitive, unspoiled
country; solitude
Services: None
Managing Agency: Bureau of Land Management: Grand Junction
Resource Area

Access: From the Visitor Center, turn left (southwest) onto
Horizon Drive. At the roundabout, continue traveling southwest.
Follow the signs for the Colorado National Monument by turning
left (south) on 7th Street, and then right (west) on Grand Avenue.
Pass through a major intersection with Highways 6 and 50 and
cross the Colorado River. Grand Avenue is now Highway 340. Turn
left on Monument Road. Travel approximately 3.5 miles to the east
entrance to the Colorado National Monument. Continue driving
up Rim Rock Drive for approximately 4 miles. Turn left (south) at
the sign indicating the road to Glade Park Store. This is East Glade
Park Road/DS Road. Travel along this road for 6 miles until you
reach the Glade Park Store. Turn right on 16½ Road and take it
for 0.6 mile until you reach BS Road (unmarked.) Turn left (west)
and travel on this maintained gravel road (which eventually turns
to dirt) past the trailhead for Knowles Canyon for approximately
15 miles. The locked gate serves as the trailhead.

Hiking in Knowles Canyon

Trail Description: Hike along an old dirt road through the rolling uplands marked by the scent of sage, piñon, and juniper. Enjoy the view to the south overlooking the Little Dolores Canyon. Pass through a barbed wire gate and be sure to close it. After hiking for approximately 3 miles, a BLM sign directs hikers off the main dirt road to the right (northwest). A gradual descent for approximately 0.5 mile leads to the Jones Canyon Overlook, complete with sweeping canyon views. There is no trail leading to the canyon floor; private property also prevents access from the Colorado River.

Knowles Canyon *** (Lower Access)

Maps: BLM Colorado Canyons National Conservation Area map;
BLM Colorado River Ruby/Horsethief Canyons map;
USGS 7.5 minute maps: Sieber Canyon, Westwater,
Bittercreek Well
Location: 30 miles from the Grand Junction Visitor Center

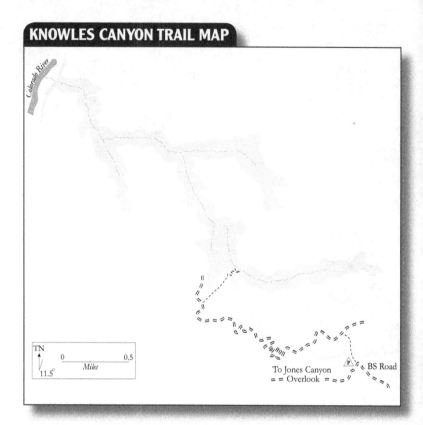

KNOWLES CANYON TRAIL MAP

Elevation Range: 5,480—6,300 feet. (Elevation at the mouth of the canyon along the Colorado River is 4,400 feet)
Length of Hike (round trip): 7 miles
Difficulty Rating: Moderate
Seasons to Hike: Spring, summer, and fall
Special Features: Deep sandstone canyon, solitude
Services: None
Managing Agency: Bureau of Land Management: Grand Junction Resource Area

Access: From the Visitor Center, turn left (southwest) onto Horizon Drive. At the roundabout, continue traveling southwest. Follow the signs for the Colorado National Monument by turning left (south) onto 7th Street, and then right (west) onto Grand Avenue. Pass through a major intersection with Highways 6 and 50 and cross the Colorado River. Grand Avenue is now Highway 340. Turn left onto Monument Road. Travel approximately 3.5

miles to the east entrance of the Colorado National Monument. Continue driving up Rim Rock Drive for approximately 4 miles. Turn left (south) at the sign indicating the road to Glade Park Store. This is East Glade Park Road/DS Road. Travel along this road for 6 miles until you reach the Glade Park Store. Turn right on 16½ Road and take it for 0.6 mile until you reach BS Road (unmarked.) Turn left (west) and travel on this maintained gravel road; eventually it turns to dirt for approximately 11.5 miles to the Upper Knowles Canyon trailhead.

Trail Description: Follow the northbound trail along the tan-and-salmon-colored Entrada Sandstone until you see a cairn on the left. Follow the path up and over the rim (west) through the rolling piñon-juniper forest. Continue to a BLM sign on an old dirt road. Follow the sign by turning left (west) onto the road. This road leads hikers around the rim of Knowles Canyon. The trail eventually descends into one of the many fingers of Knowles Canyon. After hiking a couple of miles, you will see a BLM trail sign indicating that the rim is 1 mile away. Take the footpath located to the right of the dirt road. At the rim, take in the views of the imposing Wingate Sandstone walls, spires, and arches. From the rim, the trail continues, descending steeply to the canyon floor. Those who wish to explore more of this scenic canyon should plan a backpacking trip.

Alternative Access and Routes: A river float through Horsethief and Ruby Canyons on the Colorado River provides assess to Knowles Canyon. From the Loma Boat Launch, the mouth of Knowles Canyon is 18 miles on river left, approximately 2 miles below Black Rocks.

Mee Canyon*** (Lower Access)

Maps: BLM Colorado Canyons National Conservation Area map;
　　　　BLM Colorado River-Ruby/Horsethief Canyons map;
　　　　USGS 7½ minute maps: Battleship Rock, Ruby Canyon
Location: 28 miles from the Grand Junction Visitor Center
Elevation Range: 5,500—6,780 feet
Length of Hike (round trip): 5 miles to the canyon floor and back

MEE CANYON TRAIL MAP

Colorado River

TN
11.5°

0   0.5
Miles

Huge Undercut

Difficulty Rating: Difficult; sheer exposure, scrambling, some route finding

Seasons to Hike: Spring, summer, and fall

Special Features: Scenic canyon; massive alcove; intricate route; solitude

Services: None

Managing Agency: Bureau of Land Management: Grand Junction Resource Area

Access: From the Visitor Center, turn left (southwest) onto Horizon Drive. At the roundabout, continue traveling southwest. Follow the signs for the Colorado National Monument by turning left (south) on 7th Street, and then right (west) on Grand Avenue. Pass through a major intersection with Highways 6 and 50 and cross the Colorado River. Grand Avenue is now Highway 340. Turn left on Monument Road. Travel approximately 3.5 miles to the east entrance of the Colorado National Monument. Continue driving along scenic Rim Rock Drive for approximately 11.8 miles and turn left onto a gravel road. Drive for 0.2 mile to the Black Ridge

Hiking in Mee Canyon

Hunter Access Road. There are two access roads: The Upper Access Road is open from April 15 through August 15; the Lower Access Road is open from August 15 to February 15. Both roads are closed between February 15 and April 15. A high-clearance vehicle is necessary to travel on the Upper Access Road to the Mee Canyon trailhead. Drive up the dirt road for approximately 1.5 miles until a fork is reached. Bear left onto Upper Bench Road and follow the BLM public access signs. Continue for about 6 miles, then take the left fork and follow the signs for Mee Canyon. At the last fork in the road, bear right, following the signs for Mee Canyon, and park at the trailhead sign.

Trail Description: Hike down an old dirt road through rolling grasslands and piñon-juniper country. Eventually, hikers will spot cairns to the left. No true "trail" descends into the canyon. Because of the many exposed sections, hikers must skirt along narrow sandstone ledges. Some scrambling down ledges is also involved in negotiating the descent through the cliffbands. The brilliant red canyon walls, lush vegetation along the water, and primitive nature of Mee Canyon reward hikers with solitude and spectacular scenery. When you reach the canyon bottom, head upstream a short distance to a large undercut at the base of the Wingate Sandstone. This alcove is approximately 300 feet wide, 320 feet deep, and almost 200 feet high.

Alternative Routes and Access: Although the Upper Access Road is open from April 15 through August 15 only, the Lower Access Road is open from August 15 through February 15. This road requires a high-clearance vehicle to reach the gate connecting the upper and lower access roads. Beyond this point, you will need a four-wheel drive vehicle to continue down the Lower Access Road. Park near the locked gate, hike around it and up the road to the Mee Canyon trailhead. The mouth of Mee Canyon is 13.7 miles down stream from the Loma Boat Launch and is easily accessible from the Colorado River.

Pollack Canyon/Pollack Bench Loop **

Maps: BLM Colorado Canyons National Conservation Area map;
        USGS 7½ minute maps: Mack, Battleship Rock
Location: 16 miles from the Grand Junction Visitor Center
Elevation Range: 4,500—5,200 feet
Length of Hike (round trip): From 3 to 8 miles
Difficulty Rating: Moderate
Seasons to Hike: Spring, fall, and winter
Special Features: Stunning canyon; views
Services: Restrooms at trailhead
Managing Agency: Bureau of Land Management: Grand Junction
        Resource Area

Access: Travel west on I-70 toward Fruita for approximately 12 miles. Take Exit 19 (Highway 340) and turn left (south) at the stop sign. This is also the road to take for the west entrance to the Colorado National Monument. Follow the road for about 1 mile to Kings View Estates. A sign is posted for Horsethief Canyon Wildlife Area. Turn right (west) onto Kings View Road. Within 1 mile, bear right at the fork in the road and travel for 2.2 miles. On the left side of the road, a large parking area is designated for the Pollack Bench trailhead.

POLLACK CANYON TRAIL MAP

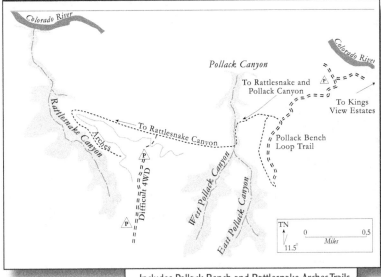

Includes Pollack Bench and Rattlesnake Arches Trails

Trail Description: From the trailhead, follow a dirt road up to the Pollack Bench. After hiking about 1.5 miles, you will see a junction marked by a BLM sign. Head west, following the sign for Pollack Canyon and Rattlesnake Arches. The Pollock Bench Loop is described below as an alternative. The next BLM sign warns of steep, rocky sections. Hike down this steep section and look for the Rattlesnake Arches trail sign. Follow this trail as it traverses a sandstone ledge. The trail eventually drops into Pollack Canyon down a steep, rocky ledge. Follow one more BLM sign for Rattlesnake Arches. After that, instead of taking the path west and out of the canyon, stay in the canyon and head south. That path will lead to the Old Ute Indian Trail and ultimately to Rattlesnake Arches. Continue up canyon until you reach the confluence of East Pollack and West Pollack. Both are beautiful, narrow canyons and offer opportunities to explore.

Alternative Route: The Pollack Bench Loop is an additional option. From the trailhead, hike 1.5 miles to the first junction and follow the sign for the Pollack Bench Loop. The loop is roughly 3.5 miles and skirts the rim of Flume Canyon to the east and Pollack Canyon to the west.

Rattlesnake Arches ***

Maps: BLM Colorado Canyons National Conservation Area map;
      BLM Colorado River-Ruby/Horsethief Canyons map;
      USGS 7½ minute maps: Mack, Battleship Rock
Location: 16 miles from the Grand Junction Visitor Center
Elevation Range: 4,500—5,420 feet
Length of Hike (round trip): 14 miles
Difficulty Rating: Moderate to strenuous
Seasons to Hike: Spring, fall, winter
Special Features: One of the largest concentration of natural
      arches in the world; spectacular scenery; solitude
Services: Restrooms at Pollack Bench trailhead
Managing Agency: Bureau of Land Management: Grand Junction
      Resource Area

Access: Rattlesnake Arches has several access routes. The following describes access from Pollack Bench; two other means of access are described in detail at the end of this description of Rattlesnake Arches. To reach the Pollack Bench trailhead, travel west on I-70 toward Fruita for approximately 12 miles. Take Exit 19 (Highway 340) and turn left (south) at the stop sign. This is also the road to take for the west entrance to the Colorado National Monument. Follow the road for about 1 mile to Kings View Estates. A sign is posted for Horsethief Canyon Wildlife Area. Turn right (west) onto Kings View Road. Within 1 mile, bear right at the fork. Travel for 2.2 miles. On the left side of the road, a large parking area is designated for the Pollack Bench trailhead.

Trail Description: From the trailhead, follow a dirt road up to the Pollack Bench. After hiking about 1.5 miles, you will reach a junction marked by a BLM sign. Head west, following the sign for Pollack Canyon and Rattlesnake Arches. The next BLM sign warns of steep, rocky sections. At this point, hikers begin their traverse through the Pollack Canyon drainages, hiking and scrambling through a few short, steep sections. Follow the signs for Rattlesnake Arches, taking the path west and out of Pollack Canyon. The trail picks up the Old Ute Indian Trail and eventually climbs steeply to the majestic uplands. Soon, you will reach the Rattlesnake Arches Loop Trail; this trail covers about 2 miles. The

Hiking the Rattlesnake Arches Trail

right fork, Lower Arches Trail, hugs the Entrada sandstone wall. Numerous arches come into view at the southwest side of the wall. To complete the loop, climb the trail through Rainbow Arch. Hikers will approach a steep sandstone wall with a few moquisteps at the bottom. If hikers are not comfortable ascending this steep wall through the arch, they can backtrack instead; the hike will be lengthened by about 1 mile.

Alternative Access and Routes: There are two additional ways to access the Rattlesnake Arches. From the Upper trailhead, a four-wheel drive vehicle is required (or a mountain bike.) A boat or canoe is needed to access the arches from the Colorado River.

Access and Route from the Colorado River—Lower Rattlesnake Canyon Trail: From the Loma Boat Launch, a 3.3-mile river float through Horsethief and Ruby Canyons on the Colorado River provides access to the mouth of Rattlesnake Canyon. The steep and strenuous route is 6 miles round trip. Follow the canyon streambed. Look for the first steep drainage on the left side of the canyon and hike up the faint game trails until you connect with the Rattlesnake Arches Loop Trail. Route finding may be difficult.

Access and Route from the Upper Trailhead—Upper Arches Trail: Note that because road conditions become wet and dangerous, access is denied from February 15 through April 15. (The BLM locks the gates several miles before the trailhead.) Travel west on I-70 toward Fruita for approximately 12 miles. Take Exit 19 (Highway 340) and turn left (south) at the stop sign. Follow the road to the west entrance of the Colorado National Monument. Follow the road for approximately 11 miles from the entrance station to the turn-off for Glade Park Store. Turn right and travel 0.2 mile to the Black Ridge Hunter Access Road. Travel 13 miles on this road, which eventually will require a four-wheel drive and high-clearance vehicle. From the trailhead, hike about 0.5 mile until you reach the Rattlesnake Arches Loop Trail.

CHAPTER 3

Hiking Winter Flats Road

Book Cliffs & Little Bookcliffs

Within the Book Cliffs there is an area called the Little Bookcliffs. The Little Bookcliffs are home to the Little Bookcliffs Wild Horse Range which is one of three wild-horse preserves in the United States. Hikers will very likely see wild horses in Main Canyon, Coal Canyon, and in the open glades atop the Tellerico Trail. The wild horses add an interesting element to hiking. Because the horses have created numerous trails on their own accord, hikers may become confused. An interesting animal behavior to observe in the Little Bookcliffs is that of stud piles. Dominant male horses (stallions) mark their territory by defecating along established boundaries, and some of these stud piles grow remarkably large. You are assured of seeing them when you venture into the Little Bookcliffs.

The Book Cliffs and Little Bookcliffs offer abundant solitude for hikers. The land is composed of deep V-cut tan-colored sandstone

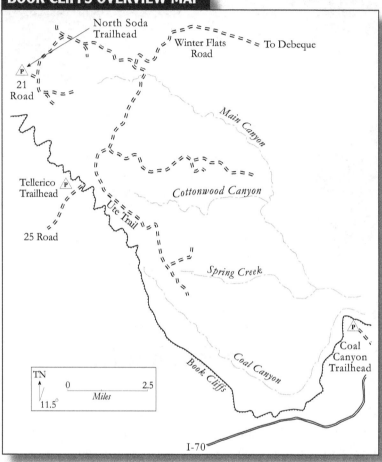

BOOK CLIFFS OVERVIEW MAP

North Soda
Trailhead

Winter Flats
Road

To Debeque

21
Road

Main Canyon

Tellerico
Trailhead

Cottonwood Canyon

Ute Trail

25 Road

Spring Creek

Coal
Canyon
Trailhead

Book Cliffs

Coal Canyon

TN

0   2.5
Miles

11.5°

I-70

canyons, perennial streams, and various springs. Hoodoos, self-standing sandstone pillars, spires, and sand-castle-like sculptures created by nature, are another special attraction of the Little Bookcliffs. Spring Creek offers the best viewing of hoodoos.

A portion of the Book Cliffs is being managed as a wilderness study area. As mentioned in the introduction, wilderness status may be obtained if there is active support for it. A drive or hike through this area helps visitors understand why this area is being studied as wilderness. The upper region of Winter Flats Road meanders through rock formations resembling those of Bryce Canyon in Utah.

Hiking in Cottonwood Canyon

The Book Cliffs and Little Bookcliffs offer several day-hikes. A suggested trip entails hiking up the Tellerico Trail. From the rim, traverse the Ute Trail road to Cottonwood Campground and Monument Rocks. Continue down the Cottonwood Trail to Main Canyon; from Main Canyon, exit to the Main Canyon trailhead. There hikers have the option of exploring the hoodoos in Spring Canyon. Backpackers must be concerned with water in this area. The springs and perennial streams offer abundant water; however, finding these water sources can sometimes be difficult.

Cottonwood Canyon **

Maps: BLM Little Bookcliffs Wild Horse Area map; USGS 7.5 minute maps: Round Mountain, Wagon Track Ridge, Winter Flats
Location: 64 miles from the Grand Junction Visitor Center
Elevation Range: 5,400—6,650 feet
Length of Hike (round trip): 6 miles
Difficulty Rating: Moderate
Seasons to Hike: Spring, summer, fall
Special Features: Wild horses; scenic canyon
Services: None

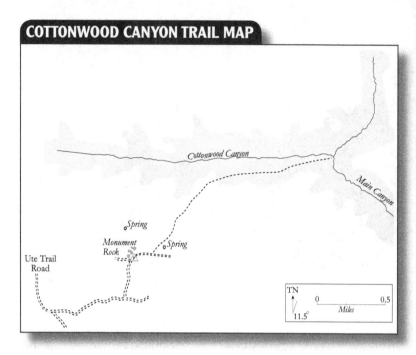

COTTONWOOD CANYON TRAIL MAP

Managing Agency: Bureau of Land Management: Grand Junction Resource Area

Access: Travel east on Interstate 70 toward Glenwood Springs approximately thirty miles to the DeBeque exit (Exit 62) and turn left at the stop sign. Follow the road over the highway, across the Colorado River, and under a train overpass. Turn left into the little town of DeBeque. At the first stop sign in town, turn left onto Minter Avenue and follow the signs for Winter Flats. Turn right onto Winter Flats Road and continue following BLM signs for the Wild Horse Area. This road requires a high-clearance vehicle. Although this dirt road to the trailhead is about 30 miles, the going is very slow and somewhat dependent upon the road conditions. Camping at Monument Rocks (the Cottonwood Canyon trailhead) is recommended. Or, consider an alternative route described in detail below. Take Winter Flats Road for about 3.4 miles to a fork in the road. The right fork leads to Coon Hollow. Take the left fork and follow the signs for the Wild Horse Area. About 15.5 miles from the Coon Hollow junction, turn left toward the Indian Park entrance. Drive 5 miles and turn right, following the sign for Monument Rocks. Travel 7.5 miles to Monument Rocks.

Trail Description: The Monument Rocks sign is located at a fork in the road. Hike northeast down the right fork in the dirt road for a few minutes until locating the Cottonwood Canyon trailhead sign. Take the trail down and north through a thick forested area and across steep slickrock. Within less than 0.5 mile, look for the Aspen Spring, which is situated in a small grove of aspen trees and surrounded by interesting rock formations. Continue along the trail as it skirts the rim of Cottonwood Canyon and ultimately drops down to the confluence of Cottonwood and Main Canyons. This is a good place to turn back. Hikers may continue down Main Canyon or head north through a gate to reach Round Mountain. The confluence of Main Canyon and Spring Creek Canyon is about 3 miles down Main Canyon. The summit of Round Mountain is approximately 1.5 miles from the confluence.

Alternative Access and Route: If a long haul down a dirt road does not sound appealing, another option is to combine Main Canyon and Cottonwood Canyon into one 14-mile round trip hike, beginning at the trailhead for Main Canyon, Hoodoo/Spring Creek Loop, and Spring Creek. This is an easy 16-mile drive from Grand Junction along I-70 to the Cameo exit.

Demaree Canyon

Maps: USGS 7.5 minute map: Howard Canyon
Location: 23 miles from the Grand Junction Visitor Center
Elevation Range: 5,200—5,800 feet
Length of Hike (round trip): 6 miles
Difficulty Rating: Moderate
Seasons to Hike: Spring, fall, and winter
Special Features: Primitive, unspoiled area
Services: None
Managing Agency: Bureau of Land Management: Grand Junction
     Resource Area

Access: Travel west on I-70 for approximately 17 miles and take exit 15 (Highway 139). This is also the Highline Lake State Park and Loma/Rangely exit. Turn right (north) at the stop sign and follow Highway 139. Pass the Mesa County/Garfield County line,

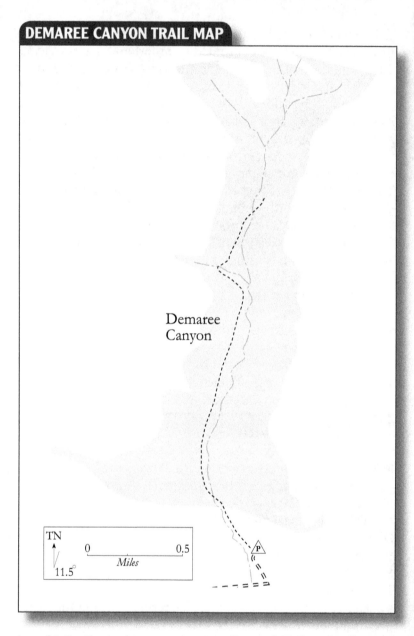

Demaree
Canyon

TN
11.5°
0   0.5
Miles

P

travel 1.5 miles and turn west onto a dirt road. Follow the dirt road west, immediately crossing a cattle guard, then look for a stock pond on the left. Veer right around a stock corral and then cross the East Salt Creek. This creek has water running through it year round. A high-clearance vehicle is necessary to cross this creek

Hiking in Demaree Canyon

and to pass through a couple of steep sections farther down the road. In fact, the road may be impassible in the winter or spring due to precipitation. After crossing the creek, travel 0.5 mile and veer left at the fork in the road. Shortly thereafter, veer right at the next fork. This road heads directly toward Demaree Canyon. Immediately cross the pipeline road and continue straight ahead. Travel 1 mile to a small parking area and the trailhead.

Trail Description: The Book Cliffs form the southern boundary of this rugged canyon country rising through pinon-juniper woodlands. Follow the streambed of Demaree Canyon north past the winding, soft sandstone walls. This incredible desert ecosystem offers excellent opportunities for solitude. There are abundant signs of wildlife, including mountain lions, hawks, and mule deer.

Hunter Canyon

Maps: USGS 7.5 minute map: Corcoran Peak
Location: 23 from the Grand Junction Visitor Center
Elevation Range: 5,400—5,800 feet

HUNTER CANYON TRAIL MAP

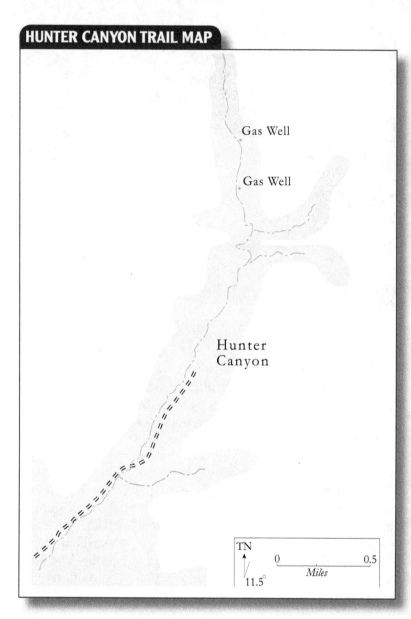

Gas Well

Gas Well

Hunter
Canyon

TN
11.5°

0   0.5
Miles

Length of Hike (round trip): The length is variable. A
recommended hike described below is about 6 miles.
Difficulty Rating: Moderate
Seasons to Hike: All seasons
Special Features: Deep, winding canyon
Services: None

Hiking in Hunter Canyon

Managing Agency: Bureau of Land Management: Grand Junction Resource Area

Access: Travel west on I-70 for approximately 6 miles. Take Exit 26 (Highways 6 & 50). At the stop sign, turn right and travel west on Highways 6 & 50 for 1 mile. Turn right onto 21 Road. Follow 21 Road north toward the Book Cliffs. Drive past a natural gas plant on the left, and shortly the road turns to gravel. The road literally leads into Hunter Canyon. Travel along the dirt road for approximately 5 miles, past the Hy Grade Mine on the cliff to the left, and park.

Trail Description: The Little Salt Wash drains through Hunter Canyon from the Roan Cliffs. Follow the creek up the canyon for a little more than 2 miles. At this point, hikers will find themselves in the midst of a unique serpentine section of the canyon. To the right, note the tributary, which has a large chock stone at its mouth. Scramble over the chock stone and explore this fork as it takes hikers through deep undercut banks. Within 0.25 mile, there is an impassible pool drop. Turn back to the main drainage and continue on up for 0.5 mile to an old oil and gas road and the first of two gas wells. This is good point to head back.

Hiking in Hoodoo/Spring Creek

Hoodoo/Spring Creek Trail Loop

Maps: BLM Little Bookcliffs Wild Horse Area map; USGS 7.5
minute maps: Cameo, Round Mountain
Location: 16 miles from the Grand Junction Visitor Center
Elevation Range: 5,000—6,600 feet
Length of Hike (round trip): 14-mile loop
Difficulty Rating: Difficult; route-finding skills required
Seasons to Hike: Spring, summer, and early fall
Special Features: Wild horses; unique geology
Services: None
Managing Agency: Bureau of Land Management: Grand Junction
Resource Area

Access: Travel east on Interstate 70 toward Glenwood Springs.
Within 14 miles, take the Cameo exit (Exit 46) and turn left at the
stop sign. Follow the road under the highway and as it turns to the
right. The road veers left across the Colorado River, crosses the
train tracks, and passes the Public Service Company plant. Cross
another bridge and the road turns to gravel. Continue on the
gravel road and veer right at the fork. The road curves to the left

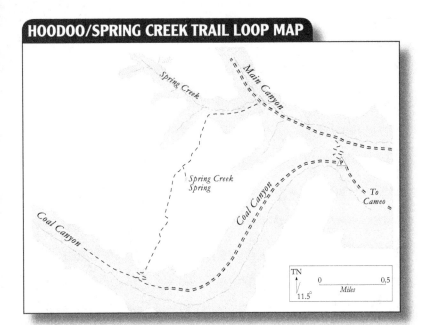

and at the next fork, bear left. Pass the BLM public access sign and part at the trailhead. This is the trailhead for Main Canyon, Spring Creek Canyon, Coal Canyon, and the Hoodoo Trail. Here there is a gate, but it is locked from December until June to protect the winter-stressed mule deer and the wild horses during the foaling season. When the gate is unlocked, motorized traffic is allowed up part of Coal Canyon and Main Canyon.

Trail Description: This long hike is suitable for experienced hikers seeking a challenge and a long day. Follow the dirt road through Coal Canyon for approximately 3 miles. Watch for wild horses on the steep hillsides on the south side of this canyon. When a sign for the Hoodoo Trail is reached, turn right (northwest) and follow the trail along the right side of the canyon for about 2 miles. Keep to the right. After passing a stock pond, look for a Hoodoo Trail sign on the left. Follow the path to the left down and across the wash. After seeing 3 hoodoos, round a bend and look for a steep trail up the hillside to the right (east). This is the last segment of the Hoodoo Trail. As the trail climbs steeply out of Coal Canyon and up onto the ridge, it passes through a beautiful band of sandstone. The top of the ridge affords great views to the south, including the back side of Mt. Garfield, the San Juan

Hiking in Spring Creek Canyon

Mountains, the Grand Mesa, and the Uncompahgre Plateau. On this ridge, look for the Hoodoo Trail to the right (east). Follow it to the northeast along the ridge. For a short way, there are a few green BLM signs and orange diamonds nailed to trees to guide hikers. When the signs disappear, the trail also becomes faint. Follow horse and deer tracks through the pinyon-juniper forest in a northeastern direction, gradually descending to Spring Creek Spring—marked by a stock tank. From here, backtrack a short distance and pick up the trail that leads down to Spring Creek. Note that the trail was washed out several years ago by severe flooding. Another option is to follow the drainage below the spring to Spring Creek. If you follow the drainage, you will encounter a couple of large spillovers that are fairly easy to get around by traveling high on either side. The last spillover presents more of a challenge; you need to abandon the drainage and head along the right side of the steep canyon until you reach large boulders and a steep talus slope. Carefully scramble down the steep scree slope to the bottom of Spring Creek. Once in the creek, the going is easy. Spring Creek is home to a fabulous display of hoodoos. Pass one tributary on the right (southeast) before reaching Main Canyon, overseen by impressive sandstone cliffs. Head southeast down Main Canyon for about 1 mile to a steep trail that leads through a notch separating Main and Coal Canyons. Follow this path back to the trailhead.

Spring Creek Canyon To Falls**

Maps: BLM Little Bookcliffs Wild Horse Area map; USGS 7.5 minute map: Cameo, Round Mountain
Location: 16 miles from the Grand Junction Visitor Center
Elevation Range: 5,000—5,800 feet
Length of Hike (round trip): 8 miles
Difficulty Rating: Moderate
Seasons to Hike: Spring, fall, and winter
Special Features: Wild horses; unique geology
Services: None
Managing Agency: Bureau of Land Management: Grand Junction Resource Area

Access: Travel east on Interstate 70 toward Glenwood Springs. Within 14 miles, take the Cameo exit (Exit 46) and turn left at the stop sign. Follow the road under the highway and as it turns to the right. The road veers left across the Colorado River, crosses the train tracks, and passes the Public Service Company plant. Cross another bridge and the road turns to gravel. Continue up the gravel road and veer right at the fork. The road curves to the left and at the next fork, bear left. Pass the BLM public access sign and part at the trailhead. This is the trailhead for Main Canyon, Spring Creek Canyon, Coal Canyon, and the Hoodoo Trail.

Trail Description: From the parking area, pass through the gate. Follow the sign for Spring Creek Trail on the right (northeast) as it takes you through a saddle that separates Coal Canyon and Main Canyon. After 1 mile or so of hiking, turn left (west) to Spring Creek. Hike up the creek bed, which is bordered by a myriad of hoodoos. The canyon narrows and soon there will be a fork in the canyon will. Spring Creek is to the left. To the right, continue for a short distance to some seasonal waterfalls.

Main Canyon

Maps: BLM Little Bookcliffs Wild Horse Area map; USGS 7.5 minute maps: Cameo, Round Mountain
Location: 16 miles from the Grand Junction Visitor Center
Elevation Range: 5,000—5,450 feet
Length of Hike (round trip): 8 miles
Difficulty Rating: Moderate
Seasons to Hike: Spring, fall, and winter
Special Features: Wild horses
Services: None
Managing Agency: Bureau of Land Management: Grand Junction Resource Area

Access: Travel east on Interstate 70 toward Glenwood Springs. Within 14 miles, take the Cameo exit (Exit 46) and turn left at the stop sign. Follow the road under the highway and as it turns to the right. The road veers left across the Colorado River, crosses the train tracks, and passes the Public Service Company plant. Cross another bridge and the road turns to gravel. Continue along the gravel road and veer right at the fork. The road curves to the left and at the next fork, bear left. Pass the BLM public access sign

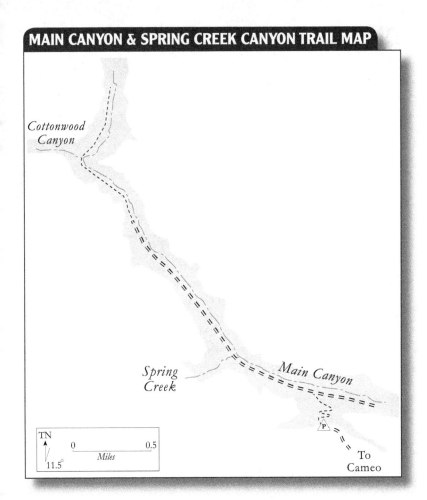

Cottonwood
Canyon

Spring
Creek

Main Canyon

TN

0   0.5
     Miles
11.5°

To
Cameo

and park at the trailhead. This is the trailhead for Main Canyon, Spring Creek Canyon, Coal Canyon, and the Hoodoo Trail.

Trail Description: From the parking area, pass through the gate; note that it is locked from December 1 until June 1 to protect the wild horses and deer from the harassment of motorized travel in Coal Canyon. Hikers and horseback riders are allowed access year round. Follow the sign for Spring Creek Trail on the right (northeast) as it rises through a saddle that separates Coal Canyon and Main Canyon. Follow the trail in a northwest direction along the trickling stream flanked by massive canyon walls. A herd of wild horses can sometimes be seen grazing in Main Canyon. After about 1 mile of hiking, you will pass the mouth of Spring

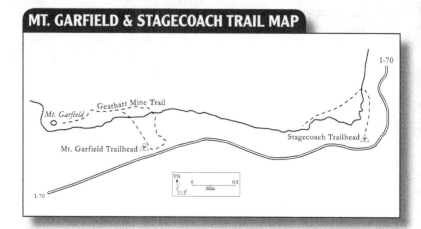

MT. GARFIELD & STAGECOACH TRAIL MAP

Creek. Continue straight up Main Canyon for 2 more miles to the junction of Main Canyon and Cottonwood Canyon. Cottonwood Canyon is on the left (west) and easily identified by a BLM sign. The right fork is the continuation of Main Canyon.

Mt. Garfield Trail *

Maps: BLM Mt. Garfield Trail Map; USGS 7.5 minute map: Mt.
     Garfield
Location: Twelve miles from the Grand Junction Visitor Center
Elevation Range: 4,740—6,740 feet
Length of Hike (round trip): 4 miles
Difficulty Rating: Strenuous
Seasons to Hike: Spring, fall, and winter. Note that the trail
     should not be traveled when wet because it is extremely
     steep.
Special Features: Views, wild horse range
Services: None
Managing Agency: Bureau of Land Management: Grand Junction
     Resource Area

Access: Travel east on I-70 toward Palisade for 10 miles and take Exit 42. At the stop sign, turn right (south) onto 37 3/10 Road. Turn at the first right (0.2 mile) onto G 7/10 Road. Head west along this road for 1.5 miles. At this point, bear right and pass under I-70 to the trailhead.

Hiking the Mt. Garfield Trail

Trail Description: To reach the trailhead, pass through the fence running east-west at the base of the Book Cliffs. The very steep trail climbs up the crest of this Book Cliff for almost 1 mile to a terrace. Watch for the wild horse herds in the early morning or evening. The trail continues, winding upward through broken sandstone and soon turns left (west.) Continue ascending at a much more moderate rate along this exposed path for about 0.5 mile. The trail then works its way up to the next terrace for an easy finish to the summit marked by a flagpole. Enjoy the views of the Grand Valley, especially the vineyards and orchards of Palisade directly below.

Alternative Route: A loop hike is possible by taking the Gearhart Mine Trail, which eventually joins the Mt. Garfield Trail. Instead of passing through the fence, head east from the parking area along a dirt road for a short distance to an unmarked trail. Climb up the steep trail as it winds through the lower Book Cliffs. As you gain elevation, look for the remains of the mine below the first rim and to the west. Pass through a small notch at the first rim and then bear left (west) and up through a rocky section to a bend in a jeep trail. Head left (west) along the bench until the trail joins Mt. Garfield trail.

Stagecoach Trail

Maps: USGS 7.5 minute map: Mt. Garfield
Location: 16 miles from the Grand Junction Visitor Center
Elevation Range: 4,700—6,500 feet
Length of Hike (round trip): 5 miles
Difficulty Rating: Moderate
Seasons to Hike: Spring, fall, and winter
Special Features: Scenic views of the Grand Valley
Services: None
Managing Agency: Bureau of Land Management: Grand Junction
      Resource Area

Access: Travel east on Interstate 70 toward Glenwood Springs. Within 11 miles, you will see the trail on the other side of the highway (north.) To access the trailhead, continue east on the highway for 2.5 miles and take the Cameo exit (Exit 46). Turn left at the stop sign. Follow the road under the highway and turn left, back onto I-70 traveling west. Travel for about 2 miles. The parking area is immediately after a caution sign for a curve.

Trail Description: Follow the steep trail up through a rocky notch. The trail levels out as it bears to the left (west). Continue through the piñon-juniper country until the trail eventually skirts along a soft sandstone rim. At the fork in the trail, take the left option. Soon the trail all but disappears, but the terminus is marked by a flagpole at a high point. Pick a path to the flagpole. Once there, you will enjoy great views overlooking the Grand Valley.

Tellerico Loop Trail ** (To Top of the Book Cliffs)

Maps: BLM Little Bookcliffs Wild Horse Area map; USGS 7.5
      minute map: Corcoran Point, Round Mountain, Winter
      Flats
Location: 15 miles from the Grand Junction Visitor Center
Elevation Range: 5,700—7,350 feet
Length of Hike (round trip): Approximately a 14-mile loop
Difficulty Rating: Difficult—steep ascent of the Book Cliffs; some
      route finding involved to complete the loop

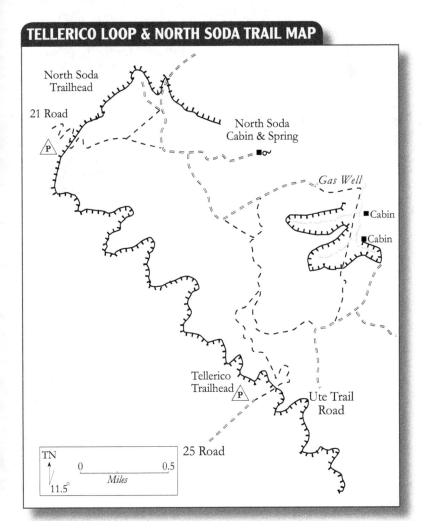

North Soda Trailhead

21 Road

North Soda Cabin & Spring

Gas Well

Cabin

Cabin

Tellerico Trailhead

Ute Trail Road

25 Road

TN
0   0.5
Miles
11.5°

Seasons to Hike: Spring, summer, and fall
Special Features: Wild horses; geology; scenic views
Services: None
Managing Agency: Bureau of Land Management: Grand Junction Resource Area

Access: Travel west on Interstate 70 for 4 miles to Exit 28 and 24 Road. At the stop light, turn right (north) onto 24 Road. Within 0.5 mile, turn right (east) on H Road. Take H Road for 1 mile to 25 Road. Turn left (north) on 25 Road and head toward the Bookcliffs. After a couple of miles, you will cross a cattle guard and here the road turns to gravel. Travel along the gravel road for approximately 7 miles to a dirt parking area on the right side of the road.

Trail Description: Head north along the dirt road from the parking area as it leads to a tight canyon. Follow a trail into the canyon and travel north up the wash to a large cairn. Take the trail to the left (northwest) as it ascends up the steep face of the Book Cliffs. The trail travels up and traverses along the Book Cliffs in a northwestern direction for a couple of miles to the ridge. Once on the ridge, look for the fork, which is the beginning of the loop section and is marked by surveyor tape tied to a large juniper, as well as BLM signs nailed on the tree. This is a good area to view the wild horses. To hike the entire loop, take the left fork and hike north through the piñon-juniper country to an expanse of slickrock. Until this point, the trail is well defined. From this point forward, some route finding is necessary. A unique challenge has been created by the wild horses because they have developed their own paths to food and water sources. Travel northwest along the slickrock and look for a worn path (the slickrock will appear lighter). Pick up the trail again and take it north down to a wash. Hike up a steep section of sandstone ledges, marked by a few steps chipped away by the Ute Indians. From here, look closely for infrequent BLM signs nailed to trees as well as surveyor tape tied to tree branches. These aids will guide you to an old dirt road. When you reach the road, turn right (northeast) and descend toward an old abandoned gas well. At the gas well, a foot path leads east down a draw to Lane Gulch. Look again for surveyor tape and BLM signs nailed to trees for guidance. Travel up (south) the lush creek marked by a small grove of cottonwood trees and scrub oak to the remains of an old cabin. Continue up the creek to a fork. Bear left and hike up the stream bed to the next fork and another old cabin. Take the right fork and continue up the wash. Stay in the wash until you see BLM signs and surveyor tape on the left side of the creek bed. From here, head up the steep trail to the Ute Trail— a well-maintained dirt road. Turn right (west) onto the road for a short distance to a junction in the road; here you will see a BLM sign indicating that the Tellerico trailhead is 7.5 miles away. Take this right fork in the road for a few minutes and look for a brown BLM post on the left side of the road. The trail leads to a footpath that will complete the loop section of this trail. Follow it to the rim overlooking the Grand Valley and back track down the trail.

North Soda Trail *

Maps: USGS 7.5 minute map: Corcoran Peak
Location: 23 miles from the Grand Junction Visitor Center
Elevation Range: 5,550—7,000 feet
Length of Hike (round trip): 5 miles
Difficulty Rating: Easy within the canyon. Gaining the top of the Book Cliffs is difficult.
Seasons to Hike: Spring and fall
Special Features: Sweeping views of the Grand Valley and surrounding areas; primitive, wild setting
Services: None
Managing Agency: Bureau of Land Management: Grand Junction Resource Area

Access: Contact the BLM office to obtain permission to cross private property to access the trail. Travel west on Interstate 70 for 6 miles and turn off on Exit 26 (Highways 6 & 50). Turn right (west) at the stop light onto Highway 6. Travel west toward Fruita for 1 mile and turn right (north) onto 21 Road. Continue on 21 Road for almost 9 miles, passing a gas plant. From the point where the road turns to gravel, travel for 2.3 miles and turn right onto an unmaintained dirt road. Deep ruts may be present on this road, and wet conditions can make the road impassable. Drive eastward on for 1.5 miles to a "T" intersection. Turn right and continue 0.5 mile to another "T" intersection. Turn left at this intersection and head toward the Book Cliffs. Travel on this road for 2 miles; you will pass a cattle corral and come to a "Y" intersection. Veer left, and continue for 1 mile; park immediately after a dilapidated cattle corral.

Trail Description: From the parking area, look for cairns that mark a cattle trail dropping into the canyon wash. Hike the well-established trail along the wash for approximately 1 mile. After 1 mile, look for a sparse trail steeply winding up the east side of the canyon and gaining access to the top of the Book Cliffs. A rancher owns the property adjacent to the mouth of the canyon; this means that hikers are technically trespassing in their attempts to gain access to the canyon. To enter this canyon legally, you must ask the rancher's permission. Permission can be obtained by contacting the Grand Junction BLM office.

CHAPTER 4

Hiking Monument Canyon Trail

Colorado National Monument

The Colorado National Monument owes its very existence to the inexhaustible commitment of a man named John Otto. Otto came to the Grand Valley in 1906. He was awestruck by the natural beauty of the surrounding area and the land that is now the Colorado National Monument. Upon the inception of his discovery of these spectacular canyons, Otto embarked on a nonstop effort to establish the area as a national monument.

John Otto was a "mile-a-minute" eccentric visionary who was severely misunderstood; indeed, several times he was committed to an insane asylum. He influenced community members to join him in his vision of establishing a national monument, and in 1911 monument status was granted. John Otto became the first park manager of the monument and earned a salary of $11 a month.

Otto was driven by his extreme passion for the land. Because he also wanted others to enjoy what he cherished, he engineered numerous trails for all to enjoy. Otto's idea "for all to enjoy" is a little different from that of the typical weekend hiker today.

One of his loosely defined "trails" involved ascending the 450-ft. Independence Monument. To accomplish this, steps were chopped and holes were drilled into the rock to fabricate a ladder-type system. Today, the ladders are gone; only the drill holes and chopped steps remain. The trail is now a popular rock-climbing route. Otto's goal in establishing this route was to place an American flag atop the Independence Monument. Otto did achieve his goal, and, in the spirit of John Otto, visitors today can view that flag once a year. Every Fourth of July, local climbers ascend the spire and place the Stars and Stripes atop in all its glory.

John Otto was also a compassionate patriot. His patriotism lead to the names designated to canyons and other features of the monument. The names Independence Monument, Liberty Cap, and Sentinel Spire are examples of Otto's patriotic influence.

The Colorado National Monument contains other examples of John Otto's enthusiastic trail building that are much more practical for the normal hiker. Gold Star Canyon, for instance, is a fine canyon for hikers to get a feel for Otto's "way of thinking." Another example of Otto's engineering feats is the Serpents Trail. This enjoyable hiking trail was originally the road taken to gain access to the Glade Park area. The National Park Service calls this trail "the crookedest road in the world."

In 1927, Otto resigned from his duties as park manager. One can only imagine that his eccentricity had probably gone a little too far. He left his beloved monument and took up residence in California, never to return.

Alcove Nature Trail

Maps: NPS Colorado National Monument official map; Trails Illustrated Colorado National Monument topo map; USGS 7.5 minute map—Colorado National Monument
Location: Twenty-six miles from the Grand Junction Visitor Center.
Elevation Range: 5,790—5,900 feet

ALCOVE NATURE & BLACK RIDGE TRAIL MAP

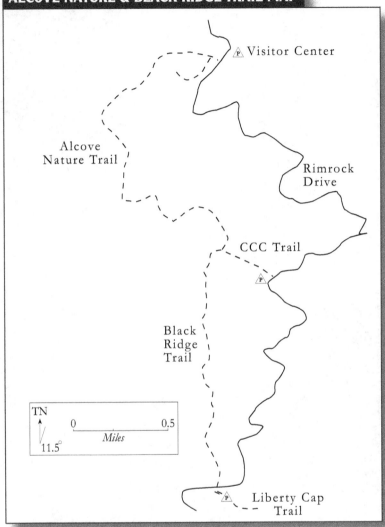

Length of Hike (round trip): 2 miles
Difficulty Rating: Easy
Seasons to Hike: All seasons
Special Features: Interpretive area; scenery
Services: Restrooms and drinking fountain at the Colorado
        National Monument Visitor Center
Managing Agency: National Park Service: Colorado National
        Monument

Hiking the Alcove Nature Trail

Access: From the Visitor Center, turn left (southwest) onto Horizon Drive. At the roundabout, continue traveling southwest. Follow the signs for the Colorado National Monument by turning left (south) onto 7th Street, and then right (west) onto Grand Avenue. Pass through a major intersection with Highways 6 and 50 and cross the Colorado River. Grand Avenue is now Highway

340. Turn left onto Monument Road. Travel approximately 3.5 miles to the east entrance to the Colorado National Monument. Follow Rim Rock Drive for approximately 18 miles to the Visitor Center. Park in the parking area.

Trail Description: Pick up a copy of the Alcove Nature Trail for 50 cents at the Visitor Center or at the trailhead. The trailhead is located on the northwest side of Rim Rock Drive, across from the Visitor Center. This self-guided nature trail gives information about many of the common plant and animal species that make their home in the monument. Follow the easy path across the Kayenta Bench to its termination in a beautiful sandstone alcove.

Black Ridge Trail

Maps: NPS Colorado National Monument official map; Trails Illustrated Colorado National Monument topo map; USGS 7.5 minute map: Colorado National Monument
Location: 23 miles from the Grand Junction Visitor Center
Elevation Range: 5,790—6,730 feet
Length of Hike (round trip): 11 miles (5.5 miles one way to the Visitor Center; 2.5 miles one way to the Civilian Conservation Corp Trail junction)
Difficulty Rating: Moderate
Seasons to Hike: All seasons
Special Features: Far-reaching views
Services: The trailhead is 6.5 miles east of the Colorado National Monument Visitor Center where drinking water and restrooms may be located.
Managing Agency: National Park Service: Colorado National Monument

Access: From the Visitor Center, turn left (southwest) onto Horizon Drive. At the roundabout, continue traveling southwest. Follow the signs for the Colorado National Monument by turning left (south) onto 7th Street, and then right (west) onto Grand Avenue. Pass through a major intersection with Highways 6 and 50 and cross the Colorado River. Grand Avenue is now Highway 340. Turn left on Monument Road. Travel approximately 3.5

miles to the east entrance to the Colorado National Monument. Continue driving along scenic Rim Rock Drive for approximately 15 miles to the trailheads serving Liberty Cap and Black Ridge.

Trail Description: Cross Rimrock Drive from the parking area to reach the trailhead. A dirt road serves as the trail and follows an old water line project. The trail, the highest one in the monument, climbs across a gently sloping grassy ridge. The scenic views extend west to the Canyonlands of Utah, south to the San Juan Mountains, and east to the Grand Valley. Hikers will also gain views of Devils Canyon.

Alternative Access and Route: The Black Ridge Trail may also be accessed from the north end of the trail at the Colorado National Monument Visitor Center. Park at the Visitor Center and cross Rim Rock Drive to pick up the trail. Another option is to hike Black Ridge Trail from the Civilian Conservation Corp (CCC) Trail. This trail is located across Rim Rock Drive from the parking area for the Coke Ovens and Monument Trail. The CCC Trail is 0.8 mile one way.

Devils Kitchen *

Maps: NPS Colorado National Monument official map; Trails Illustrated Colorado National Monument topo map; USGS 7.5 minute map: Colorado National Monument
Location: 8 miles from the Grand Junction Visitor Center
Elevation Range: 5,060—5,400 feet
Length of Hike (round trip): 1.5 miles
Difficulty Rating: Easy to the base of the monolith; moderate climb thereafter
Season to Hike: All seasons
Special Features: Natural sandstone grotto; great spot for a picnic
Services: Picnic area across from the parking area for hikers
Managing Agency: National Park Service: Colorado National Monument

Access: From the Visitor Center, turn left (southwest) onto Horizon Drive. At the roundabout, continue traveling southwest.

Follow the signs for the Colorado National Monument by turning left (south) onto 7th Street, and then right (west) onto Grand Avenue. Pass through a major intersection with Highways 6 and 50 and cross the Colorado River. Grand Avenue is now Highway 340. Turn left onto Monument Road. Travel approximately 3.5 miles to the east entrance of the Colorado National Monument. Almost immediately after entry into the monument, hikers will approach the parking area on the left side of the road.

Trail Description: The trailhead is located at the south end of the parking area. Follow the trail as it descends toward a wash. Within a few minutes a trail junction and sign indicates that the left fork leads to Devils Kitchen. Continue hiking, cross the wash, and travel across level terrain for a few minutes. Ascend the slickrock slope following the cairns and man-made steps to the monolith— Devils Kitchen.

No Thoroughfare Canyon **

Maps: NPS Colorado National Monument official map; Trails Illustrated Colorado National Monument topo map; USGS 7.5 minute map: Colorado National Monument
Location: 8 miles from the Grand Junction Visitor Center
Elevation Range: 5,000—6,820 feet
Length of Hike (round trip): The full hike is 17 miles. A recommended hike (described below) is approximately 7 miles round trip.
Difficulty Rating: Easy to the lower falls; moderate beyond
Seasons to Hike: Spring, fall, and winter
Special Features: Waterfalls; primitive canyon; huge sandstone canyon walls
Services: Picnic area across from the parking area for hikers
Managing Agency: National Park Service: Colorado National Monument

Access: From the Visitor Center, turn left (southwest) onto Horizon Drive. At the roundabout, continue traveling southwest. Follow the signs for the Colorado National Monument by turning left (south) onto 7th Street, and then right (west) onto Grand

NO THOROUGHFARE CANYON & DEVIL'S KITCHEN TRAIL MAP

Rimrock Drive

Devils Kitchen Trail

No Thoroughfare Canyon

Falls

Falls

Little Park Road

TN
11.5°

0   0.5
Miles

Avenue. Pass through a major intersection with Highways 6 and 50 and cross the Colorado River. Grand Avenue is now Highway 340. Turn left onto Monument Road. Travel approximately 3.5 miles to the east entrance of the Colorado National Monument. Almost immediately after entering the monument, hikers will approach the parking area on the left side of the road.

Trail Description: The trailhead is located at the south end of the parking area. Follow the trail as it descends toward a wash. Within a few minutes a trail junction and a sign indicate that the right fork leads to No Thoroughfare Canyon. Beyond the Devils Kitchen area, follow the undeveloped route upstream. This remote canyon features two stunning waterfalls in its inner gorge, as well as several smaller ones. The seasonal streambed is typically dry during the warmer months and may be frozen or covered with a light layer of snow in the winter months. After hiking approximately 2 miles, hikers will come upon the first of the two prominent waterfalls. This fall cascades approximately 100 feet to a pool bordered by cottonwood trees. To continue up the drainage and around the waterfall, detour to the right up and over steep terrain. Shortly

Hiking the No Thoroughfare Canyon Trail

after reaching the head of the waterfall, hikers will encounter an obvious tributary to the left. If time permits, consider exploring this tributary; otherwise, continue upstream. Bear in mind that the vegetation becomes increasingly thick upstream. After about thirty minutes of hiking, you will encounter the second prominent waterfall, which is nearly twice as large as the first. This is a good place to turn around unless hikers are planning to make it all the way to the head of the canyon. To overcome the obstacle created by this second waterfall, look for a very steep drainage on the right as soon as the waterfall is within eyesight. As you scramble up this drainage, watch for the occasional cairn. Travel on this upper terrace through the thick sagebrush and scrub oak. When you reach the crest of the waterfall, hike back down to the streambed and continue upstream. As you approach the upper drainage, thrash through the healthy sagebrush and steep sandy ravines until you encounter a maintained trail; this trail leads to the top of the plateau.

Alternative Access and Route: Access is available at the head of No Thoroughfare Canyon for hikers choosing to travel downstream. To reach the top, follow the directions above. Instead of turning into the parking lot just beyond the east entrance of the monument, continue traveling up Rim Rock Drive for approximately 4 miles. Turn left on DS Road at the sign indicating Glade Park-Pinyon Mesa. Follow DS Road for approximately 4.5 miles and turn left on CS Road. Follow the windy road for about 1.5 miles. Look for a small gravel pullout on the left side of the road and a very small National Park Service sign.

Gold Star Canyon *

Maps: NPS Colorado National Monument official map; Trails Illustrated Colorado National Monument topo map; USGS 7.5 minute map: Colorado National Monument
Location: 11 miles from the Grand Junction Visitor Center
Elevation Range: 4,800—6,000 feet
Length of Hike (round trip): Approximately 3.5 miles
Difficulty Rating: Difficult; steep ascent; route finding required to reach the rim of Monument Mesa
Seasons to Hike: Spring, fall, and winter
Special Features: Scenic canyon; steep, intricate trail
Managing Agency: National Park Service: Colorado National Monument

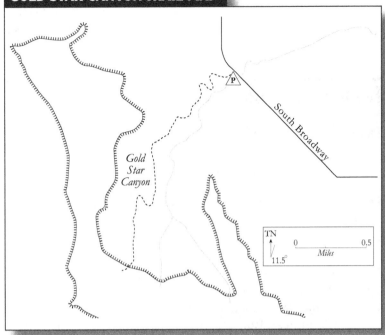

Access: From the Visitor Center, turn left (southwest) onto Horizon Drive. At the roundabout, continue traveling southwest. Follow the signs for the Colorado National Monument by turning left (south) onto 7th Street, and then right (west) onto Grand Avenue. Pass through a major intersection with Highways 6 and 50 and cross the Colorado River. Grand Avenue is now Highway 340. Pass Monument Road and continue on Highway 340 for approximately 3 miles. Turn left on South Broadway. Travel on this road for about 2.7 miles and then turn left to continue on South Broadway. Continue for approximately 2.1 miles until you see a small pullout on the left side of the road and an entrance through the NPS fence. Park here.

Trail Description: Follow the trail that skirts up and around on the right side of the dark Precambrian rock. After the steep ascent, the trail winds through the gently rolling piñon-juniper country. You will see several faint trails in this area. Keep to the right, hiking south until you see a fork in the trail. Head right and up toward the large expanse of sandstone. Cross a small ledge along the sandstone. A faint trail winds up the large sandstone wall and crosses several more ledges. Use the carved steps to scramble past several steep sections in the cliff bands. Scramble up a broken ledge to reach the rim of the Monument Mesa.

Kodels Canyon

Maps: NPS Colorado National Monument official map; Trails Illustrated Colorado National Monument topo map; USGS 7.5 minute map: Colorado National Monument, Fruita
Location: 13 miles from the Grand Junction Visitor Center
Elevation Range: 4,500—5,100 feet
Length of Hike (round trip): 3.5 miles
Difficulty Rating: Moderate
Season to Hike: Spring, fall, and winter
Special Features: Quiet and scenic red sandstone canyon
Managing Agency: National Park Service: Colorado National Monument; Bureau of Land Management: Grand Junction Resource Area

Access: Travel west on I-70 toward Fruita for approximately 12 miles. Take Exit 19 (Highway 340) and turn left (south) at the stop sign. This road also leads to the west entrance to the Colorado National Monument. Follow the road for 1.4 miles, just past Kings View Estates. A small BLM trailhead sign is posted on the right side (west) of the road. Park at this small pullout.

Trail Description: Hikers should head in a southwestern direction and down toward a wash. The trail forks in several places; at the first fork, veer to the right (southwest). Follow the BLM trail signs and head west up the wash toward Kodels Canyon. When the trail intersects with telephone lines, bear left toward the mouth of Kodels Canyon. Follow the trail as it meanders in and along the creek bed. Pass through the BLM/NPS boundary. The canyon widens and opens up to sheer Wingate Sandstone walls. Pass through the meadow-like canyon as the trail approaches the steep Precambrian rock. Bear right (west) at the fork. Climb up through the Precambrian layer to gain access to the upper reaches of this

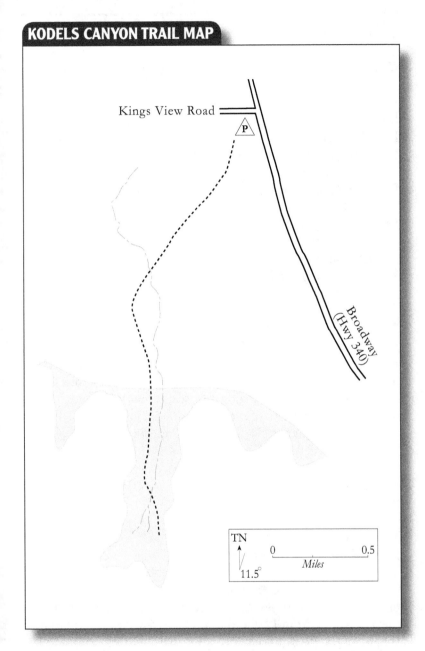

KODELS CANYON TRAIL MAP

Kings View Road

P

Broadway
(Hwy 340)

TN

11.5°

0   0.5
Miles

canyon, marked by piñon-juniper vegetation and an occasional
yucca plant or cottonwood tree. This quiet canyon is a good place
to spot wildlife, including bald eagles, mourning doves, and mule
deer.

Liberty Cap **

Maps: NPS Colorado National Monument official map; Trails
Illustrated Colorado National Monument topo map;
USGS 7.5 minute map: Colorado National Monument
Location: 9 miles from the Grand Junction Visitor Center
Elevation Range: 4,800—6,550 feet
Length of Hike (round trip): 14 miles. A recommended hike
(described below) is 5 miles.
Difficulty Rating: Moderate; however, the ascent to the uplands is
strenuous.
Seasons to Hike: Spring, fall, and winter. Steep, icy sections may
be encountered in December and January.
Special Features: Steep, intricate trail; scenic views
Managing Agency: National Park Service: Colorado National
Monument

Access: From the Visitor Center, turn left (southwest) onto
Horizon Drive. At the roundabout, continue traveling southwest.
Follow the signs for the Colorado National Monument by turning
left (south) onto 7th Street, and then right (west) onto Grand
Avenue. Pass through a major intersection with Highways 6 and
50 and cross the Colorado River. Grand Avenue is now Highway
340. Pass Monument Road and continue on Highway 340 for
approximately 3 miles. Turn left onto South Broadway. Travel on
this road for about 1 mile until you reach Wildwood Drive. Turn
left and in 0.5 mile you will reach the trailhead sign and small
parking area on the right.

Trail Description: A recommended hike will take hikers to the
rounded sandstone mound known as the Liberty Cap on the rim
of the Monument Mesa. To reach the Liberty Cap, follow the well-
established trail across rolling slopes. The trail leads to the base
of the dark Precambrian rock escarpment and ascends behind this
massive slab. Within 1.5 miles, hikers will reach a trail junction at
the top of the Precambrian formation. The left fork leads into Ute
Canyon. Take the right fork and follow the trail as it winds along
the Wingate and Kayenta Sandstone to the top of the Monument
Mesa. The mesa top affords outstanding views of the Grand Valley,
the Book Cliffs, the Grand Mesa, and a great overview of Ute

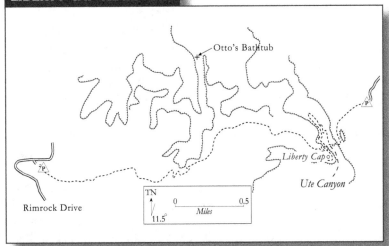

Otto's Bathtub

P

Liberty Cap

Ute Canyon

Rimrock Drive

TN

0   0.5
         Miles
11.5°

Canyon. On a clear day, the San Juan Mountains are within view. Hikers can reach the official top of the Liberty Cap by skirting around the north side of the sandstone mound to some carved steps and fixed iron. At this point, hikers will have traveled 2.5 miles and ascended over 1,000 feet.

Hikers who decide to continue on the trail should follow the easy trail across the Monument Mesa as it gently winds through sagebrush flats and the piñon-juniper forest.

Upper Liberty Cap to Otto's Bathtub

Maps: NPS Colorado National Monument official map; Trails Illustrated Colorado National Monument topo map; USGS 7.5 minute map: Colorado National Monument
Location: 20 miles from the Grand Junction Visitor Center
Elevation Range: 6,100—6,550 feet
Length of Hike (round trip): Approximately 8 miles
Difficulty Rating: Moderate
Seasons to Hike: All seasons
Special Features: Scenic views; slickrock hiking; historic sight
Managing Agency: National Park Service: Colorado National Monument

Access: From the Visitor Center, turn left (southwest) onto Horizon Drive. At the roundabout, continue traveling southwest. Follow the signs for the Colorado National Monument by turning left (south) onto 7th Street, and then right (west) onto Grand Avenue. Pass through a major intersection with Highways 6 and 50 and cross the Colorado River. Grand Avenue is now Highway 340. Turn left onto Monument Road. Travel approximately 3.5 miles to the east entrance of the Colorado National Monument. Continue driving along scenic Rim Rock Drive for approximately 11.5 miles to the trailhead for both Liberty Cap and Black Ridge.

Trail Description: Follow the easy rolling trail across the piñon-juniper forest and meadows of the Monument Mesa along the old Motor Nature Trail. In approximately 2 miles, you will see two sets of switchbacks. Shortly after hiking down this section, look on the left side of the trail for a cairn, which identifies the path to Otto's Bathtub. Follow the trail to the northern arm of Monument Mesa and travel along the Entrada slickrock, the top of smooth, rounded, salmon-pink cliffs. Continue beyond two large pools formed in the sandstone along a narrow rim of sandstone. Once the slickrock widens again, look for Otto's Bathtub over the rim on the left. Otto's Bathtub is a narrow opening that was dammed to capture runoff water. It is marked by a few carved steps and handholds that allowed access to the bottom of the small basin.

Monument Canyon ***

Maps: NPS Colorado National Monument official map; Trails
   Illustrated Colorado National Monument topo map;
   USGS 7.5 minute map: Colorado National Monument
Location: 12 miles from the Grand Junction Visitor Center
Elevation Range: 4,700—6,140 feet
Length of Hike (round trip): 12 miles
Difficulty Rating: Moderate
Seasons to Hike: Spring, fall, and winter
Special Features: Scenic canyon; spectacular Wingate Sandstone
   walls; monoliths
Services: None

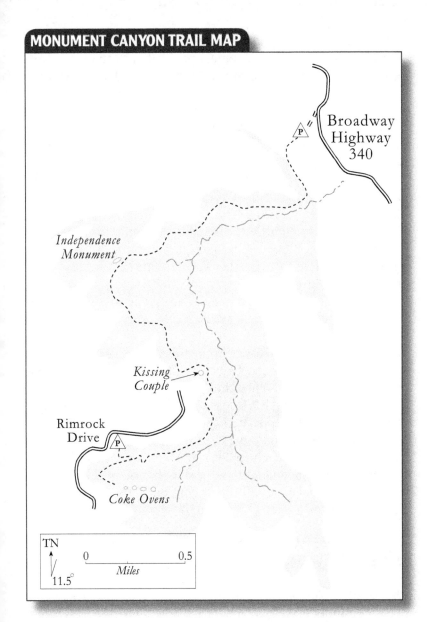

MONUMENT CANYON TRAIL MAP

Broadway
Highway
340

Independence
Monument

Kissing
Couple

Rimrock
Drive

Coke Ovens

TN
11.5°

0   0.5
Miles

Managing Agency: National Park Service: Colorado National
Monument

Access: Travel west on Interstate 70 toward Fruita for 4 miles.
Take Exit 28 and turn left onto Redlands Parkway. Travel along
Redlands Parkway for 3.5 miles to the intersection of Broadway

(Highway 340) and Redlands Parkway. Turn right (west) onto Broadway and travel for 4.5 miles. Turn left onto an easy-to-miss gravel road that shortly takes you to the trailhead parking area.

Trail Description: From the lower parking area, follow the trail bordering the small subdivision to the mouth of the canyon, which is marked by lush vegetation. The trail gradually climbs above the streambed to the towering cliffs formed by the Wingate Sandstone. After approximately 2 miles, the trail meanders among many of the canyon's bold red spires and pinnacles, the first being Independence Monument. The second monolith along the trail is Kissing Couple. Shortly after passing this spire, the trail makes a turn to the west and winds steeply up and out of the canyon, gaining more than 500 feet of elevation. Approximately 200 yards before reaching Rimrock Drive, take the left fork for a detour along the Coke Ovens Trail and a view of the massive rounded sandstone knobs—the "coke ovens."

Alternative Access and Route: From the Visitor Center, turn left (southwest) onto Horizon Drive. At the roundabout, continue traveling southwest. Follow the signs for the Colorado National Monument by turning left (south) onto 7th Street, and then right (west) onto Grand Avenue. Pass through a major intersection with Highways 6 and 50 and cross the Colorado River. Grand Avenue is now Highway 340. Turn left onto Monument Road. Travel approximately 3.5 miles to the east entrance of the Colorado National Monument. Continue driving on the scenic Rim Rock Drive for approximately 14 miles to the Monument Canyon Trail.

Red Canyon

Maps: NPS Colorado National Monument official map; USGS 7.5
    minute map: Colorado National Monument
Location: 15 miles from the Grand Junction Visitor Center
Elevation Range: 4,900—5,900 feet
Length of Hike (round trip): 6 miles
Difficulty Rating: moderate
Seasons to Hike: Spring, fall, and winter. Icy sections may be
    encountered in December and January.

Hiking in Red Canyon

Special Features: Quiet and scenic red sandstone canyon
Services: None
Managing Agency: National Park Service: Colorado National
Monument

Access: Travel west on Interstate 70 toward Fruita for 4 miles.
Take Exit 28 and turn left onto Redlands Parkway. Continue along
Redlands Parkway for 4.5 miles, passing through the intersection
of Redlands Parkway and Broadway (Highway 340). Turn left
(south) onto South Camp Road and travel for almost 2 miles. Park
alongside the road and look for a dry, braided wash.

Trail Description: Urban sprawl, narrow-minded developers, and
poor planning have made access to Red Canyon lengthier than it
needed to be. From South Camp Road, look for the dry, braided
stream bed of Red Canyon. Meander up this wash, passing between
houses. Eventually you will reach the mouth of the canyon, where

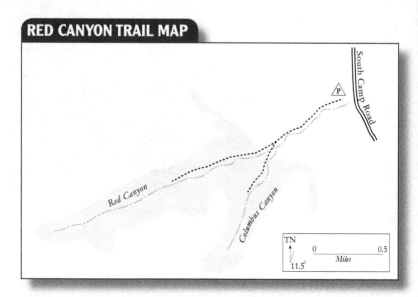

the stream begins flowing. The canyon walls become narrow and deep and you will have to navigate a few scattered spillovers.

Old Gordon Trail

Maps: NPS Colorado National Monument official map; Trails Illustrated Colorado National Monument topo map; USGS 7.5 minute map: Colorado National Monument
Location: 8 miles from the Grand Junction Visitor Center
Elevation Range: 4,980—6,620 feet
Length of Hike (round trip): 8 miles
Difficulty Rating: Moderate
Seasons to Hike: Spring, fall, and winter
Special Features: Historic trail
Services: Picnic area across from the parking area
Managing Agency: National Park Service: Colorado National Monument

Access: From the Visitor Center, turn left (southwest) onto Horizon Drive. At the roundabout, continue traveling southwest. Follow the signs for the Colorado National Monument by turning left (south) onto 7th Street, and then right (west) onto Grand Avenue. Pass through a major intersection with Highways 6 and

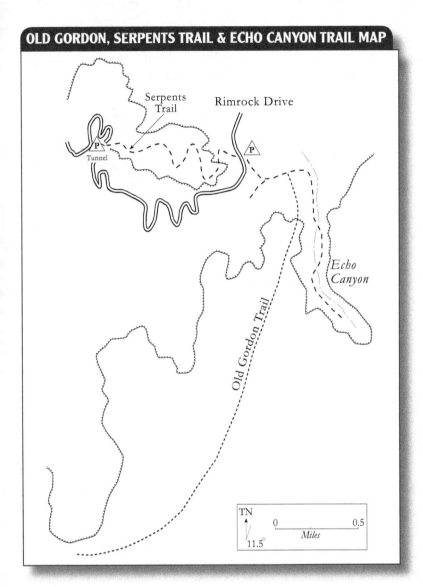

OLD GORDON, SERPENTS TRAIL & ECHO CANYON TRAIL MAP

Serpents Trail

Rimrock Drive

P

Tunnel

P

Echo Canyon

Old Gordon Trail

TN

0   0.5

Miles

11.5°

50 and cross the Colorado River. Grand Avenue is now Highway 340. Turn left onto Monument Road. Travel approximately 3.5 miles to the east entrance of the Colorado National Monument. Almost immediately after entry into the monument, hikers will approach the parking area on the left side of the road.

Trail Description: The trailhead is located at the south end of the parking area. Follow the trail as it descends toward a wash. Within a few minutes you will reach a trail junction. Take the left fork and cross the wash. After the wash, the Old Gordon Trail skirts around and up the east rim of No Thoroughfare Canyon. The trail climbs steadily over the slickrock on remaining sections of constructed berms. The route was built by early settlers to provide access to logging and cattle camps in the uplands. Follow the trail toward the high country on the south end of the monument. As you reach the top of the trail, you will find opportunities to explore as well as outstanding views of the Grand Valley, the Book Cliffs, and the Grand Mesa.

Echo Canyon *

Maps: NPS Colorado National Monument official map; Trails
        Illustrated Colorado National Monument topo map;
        USGS 7.5 minute map: Colorado National Monument
Location: 8 miles from the Grand Junction Visitor Center
Elevation Range: 4,980—5400 feet
Length of Hike (round trip): 3 miles
Difficulty Rating: Easy
Seasons to Hike: Spring, fall, and winter
Special Features: Scenic red sandstone canyon
Managing Agency: National Park Service: Colorado National
        Monument

Access: From the Visitor Center, turn left (southwest) onto Horizon Drive. At the roundabout, continue traveling southwest. Follow the signs for the Colorado National Monument by turning left (south) onto 7th Street, and then right (west) onto Grand Avenue. Pass through a major intersection with Highways 6 and 50 and cross the Colorado River. Grand Avenue is now Highway 340. Turn left on Monument Road. Travel approximately 3.5 miles to the east entrance of the Colorado National Monument. Almost immediately after entry into the monument, hikers will approach the parking area on the left side of the road.

Trail Description: The trailhead is located at the south end of the parking area. Follow the trail and signs for the Old Gordon Trail as it descends toward a wash. Cross the wash and follow the Old

Gordon Trail around and up the east rim of No Thoroughfare Canyon. Immediately before the trail climbs steadily over the slickrock, turn left onto an unmarked trail. Soon you will see a sign stating that this is private property and that no dogs or bicycles are allowed. Stay on the trail as it descends into Echo Canyon. The trail flirts with the streambed as it takes hikers through a scenic canyon bordered by Wingate Sandstone walls and lush habitat. Eventually, the trail ends in a grove of cottonwood trees at the head of this box canyon punctuated by a beautiful seasonal waterfall.

Serpents Trail

Maps: NPS Colorado National Monument official map; Trails
Illustrated Colorado National Monument topo map;
USGS 7.5 minute map: Colorado National Monument
Location: 8 miles from the Grand Junction Visitor Center
Elevation Range: 5,060—5,900 feet
Length of Hike (round trip): 4.5 miles
Difficulty Rating: Moderate
Seasons to Hike: Spring, fall, and winter
Special Features: Historic trail; scenic views
Services: Picnic area across from the parking area
Managing Agency: National Park Service: Colorado National
Monument

Access: From the Visitor Center, turn left (southwest) onto Horizon Drive. At the roundabout, continue traveling southwest. Follow the signs for the Colorado National Monument by turning left (south) onto 7th Street, and then right (west) onto Grand Avenue. Pass through a major intersection with Highways 6 and 50 and cross the Colorado River. Grand Avenue is now Highway 340. Turn left onto Monument Road. Travel approximately 3.5 miles to the east entrance to the Colorado National Monument. Almost immediately after entry into the monument, hikers will approach the parking area on the left side of the road.

Trail Description: The trailhead is located west of the parking area, across the road. This trail is popular with the locals due to the easy access and wide, moderate grade. It climbs steadily heading west, and eventually ends when it joins Rim Rock Drive. The route was engineered as a road in the early 1900s by John Otto, trail builder and founder of the Colorado National Monument. Until 1950, this was the main road into the uplands. Featuring more than fifty switchbacks, it was once called the "Crookedest Road in the World."

Alternative Access: This trail may be accessed from its upper end. Instead of parking just beyond the east entrance to the monument, continue up Rim Rock Drive for 2.5 miles. Shortly after passing through the tunnel, you will see a small parking area on the left.

Otto's Trail ***

Maps: NPS Colorado National Monument official map; Trails Illustrated Colorado National Monument topo map; USGS 7.5 minute map: Colorado National Monument
Location: 25 miles from the Grand Junction Visitor Center
Elevation Range: 5,620—5,800 feet
Length of Hike (round trip): 1 mile
Difficulty Rating: Easy
Season to Hike: All seasons
Special Features: Dramatic overlook
Services: This trailhead is 1 mile east of the Colorado National Monument Visitor Center, where hikers can get drinking water and use restrooms.
Managing Agency: National Park Service: Colorado National Monument

Access: From the Visitor Center, turn left (southwest) onto Horizon Drive. At the roundabout, continue traveling southwest. Follow the signs for the Colorado National Monument by turning left (south) onto 7th Street, and then right (west) onto Grand Avenue. Pass through a major intersection with Highways 6 and 50 and cross the Colorado River. Grand Avenue is now Highway 340. Turn left onto Monument Road. Travel approximately 3.5 miles to the east entrance of the Colorado National Monument. Continue driving along scenic Rim Rock Drive for approximately 17 miles to the trailhead.

Trail Description: This mildly sloping trail leads to a promontory overlooking several monoliths, including Pipe Organ, Sentinel Spire, and Independence Monument, as well as the canyons.

Ute Canyon ***

Maps: NPS Colorado National Monument official map; Trails Illustrated Colorado National Monument topo map; USGS 7.5 minute map: Colorado National Monument

Location: 9 miles from the Grand Junction Visitor Center

Elevation Range: 4,800—6,440 feet

Length of Hike (round trip): 14 miles

Difficulty Rating: Moderate for the most part, but the ascent to the uplands is strenuous.

Seasons to Hike: Spring, fall, and winter

Special Features: Scenic canyon; brilliant red sandstone walls

Services: None

Managing Agency: National Park Service: Colorado National Monument

Access: From the Visitor Center, turn left (southwest) onto Horizon Drive. At the roundabout, continue traveling southwest. Follow the signs for the Colorado National Monument by turning left (south) onto 7th Street, and then right (west) onto Grand Avenue. Pass through a major intersection with Highways 6 and

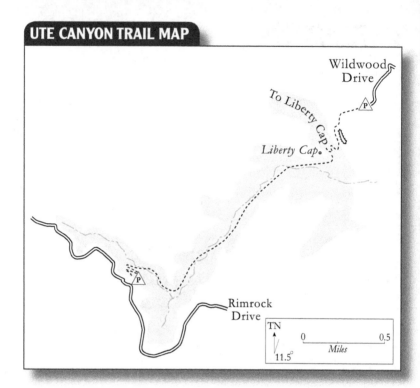

UTE CANYON TRAIL MAP

Wildwood
Drive

To Liberty Cap

Liberty Cap.

Rimrock
Drive

TN

0   0.5

Miles

11.5°

50 and cross the Colorado River. Grand Avenue is now Highway 340. Pass Monument Road and continue on Highway 340 for approximately 3 miles. Turn left onto South Broadway. Travel on this road for about 1 mile until you reach Wildwood Drive. Turn left and in 0.5 mile you will reach the trailhead sign and small parking area on the right.

Trail Description: Ute Canyon Trail and Liberty Cap Trail share the path from the trailhead to the junction on top of the Precambrian bench. To reach Ute Canyon, follow the well-established trail across the rolling slopes. The trail leads to the base of the dark Precambrian rock escarpment and ascends behind this massive slab. Within 1.5 miles, hikers will reach a trail junction at the top of the Precambrian formation. The left fork leads the way into Ute Canyon. Take this fork and follow the trail to Ute Canyon, the longest in the monument. Continue up along the seasonal stream and small pools. Black schist and gneiss form the canyon floor in the lower part of Ute Canyon. The stream is flanked by willows and lush cottonwoods. After several miles of hiking, you will reach a

Hiking in Ute Canyon

big bend. Keep to the right. Hikers can walk all the way to Suction Point, at the head of the canyon, to view a seasonal waterfall. About 1 mile before Suction Point, a maintained but strenuous trail up the talus slope on the south side of the drainage leads to the plateau and Rim Rock Drive.

Alternative Access and Route: An interesting route involves hiking from the Upper Ute Canyon trailhead to Suction Point. To reach this trailhead from the Visitor Center, turn left (southwest) onto Horizon Drive. At the roundabout, continue traveling southwest. Follow the signs for the Colorado National Monument by turning left (south) onto 7th Street, and then right (west) onto Grand Avenue. Pass through a major intersection with Highways 6 and 50 and cross the Colorado River. Grand Avenue is now Highway 340. Turn left onto Monument Road. Travel approximately 3.5 miles to the east entrance of the Colorado National Monument. Continue driving up the scenic Rim Rock Drive for approximately 8.7 miles after passing the Ute Canyon View to the trailhead. Hike down the steep constructed trail to the canyon floor. In the winter, this north-facing section of the trail may be icy and snow-packed. Instead of traveling down the streambed, head up the canyon for approximately 1 mile to Suction Point, which is a rimfall rather than a waterfall; seasonal water literally drops off into space 100 feet above the bottom of the canyon. There is no trail up to Suction Point, so hikers must work their way through thick vegetation.

Trail Notes

CHAPTER 5

Hiking Redlands Loop

City Trails & State Parks

The vast majority of city trails and state park trails are nestled along waterways. Hikers can experience wetlands habitat that is rare in the desert lands. Approximately 1 percent of all desert lands are wetlands, yet over 90 percent of all desert animals depend on that habitat for survival; it is therefore important that we preserve wetlands. Water-front trails offer hikers excellent opportunities to observe abundant wildlife. Some trails are paved (handicapped accessible), and many trails meander through groves of cottonwoods. Numerous benches are strategically placed under cottonwoods overlooking waterways; these are delightful spots where you can stop a while and ponder the mysteries of life.

The long-term goal of the city trails planning committee is to connect Palisade, Grand Junction, and Fruita via paved riverside trails. Progress is moving along, and possibly by 2010 the goal will be met.

Highline Lake State Park Loop Trail*

Maps: Colorado State Parks map: Highline Lake
Location: 25 miles from the Grand Junction Visitor Center
Elevation Range: 4,600—4,600 feet
Length of Hike (round trip): 3.5 mile loop
Difficulty Rating: Easy
Seasons to Hike: All seasons
Special Features: Birds, water sports, camping
Services: Restrooms at trailhead; camping facilities, group shelter and picnic areas, handicapped-accessible campsite, and swimming area
Managing Agency: Colorado State Parks

Access: Travel west on I-70 for approximately 17 miles and take Exit 15 (Highway 139). This is also the Highline Lake State Park and Loma/Rangely exit. Turn right (north) at the stop sign and follow Highway 139 north for approximately 5 miles. Turn left (west) onto O Road. In about 1 mile, turn right onto 11 8/10 Road and follow the signs for the picnic area. Turn left into Highline State Park and then right toward the trailhead.

Trail Description: Highline Lake State Park is a popular place to enjoy water sports in the summer. The park has two lakes— Highline Lake and Mack Mesa Lake. Highline Lake offers opportunities for recreation, including water skiing, swimming, and fishing. Mack Mesa Lake offers solitude from motorized recreation and great early-season trout fishing. In the winter, this is an excellent place to observe migratory birds, particularly ducks

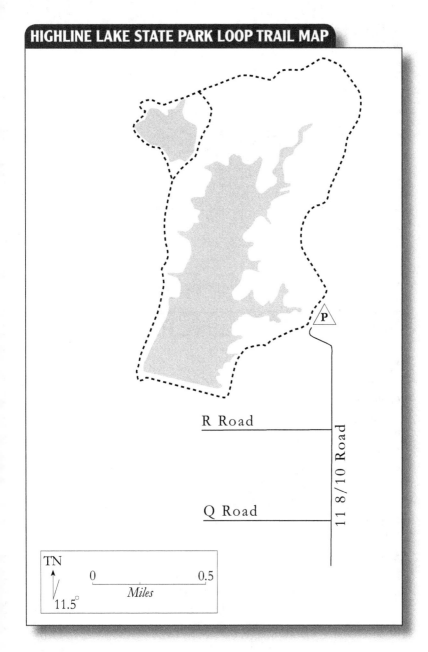

R Road

11 8/10 Road

Q Road

TN

11.5°

0   0.5

Miles

and geese, as well as such birds as the bald eagle, golden eagle, blue heron, snowy egret, white pelican, and whooping crane. The gravel loop trail accommodates hikers and mountain bike riders. The trail circles both Highline Lake and Mack Mesa Lake.

VEGA STATE PARK TRAIL MAP

Entrance Station ■

Vega Reservoir

P Cattleman Meadows

Nature Trail

TN
11.5°

0   0.5
Miles

Vega State Park Nature Trail

Maps: Colorado State Parks map: Vega
Location: 50 miles from the Grand Junction Visitor Center
Elevation Range: 8,000—8,100
Length of Hike (round trip): 4 miles
Difficulty Rating: Easy
Seasons to Hike: Summer, fall
Special Features: Outdoor recreation; subalpine ecosystem
Services: Restrooms, camping facilities, water; picnic areas with
          shelter; lodge with restaurant open seasonally
Managing Agency: Colorado State Parks

Access: Travel east on I-70 for approximately 17 miles and take
Exit 49, following the signs for Collbran. Travel 10 miles and turn
left (east) onto Highway 330. Pass through quaint Plateau City.
Turn left in the center of Collbran and follow the signs for Vega
Reservoir. Cross the bridge and take a right. Travel for 12 miles
or so to the entrance station, where a fee is collected. Turn right
(south) for a short distance to the trailhead.

Trail Description: Vega State Park is popular for trout fishing,
camping, water skiing, and hunting. The reservoir is 2 miles long

CORN LAKE TRAIL MAP

and surrounded by beautiful subalpine meadows, wild flowers, and aspen groves. The area was historically used by ranchers to graze their cattle. The Dominguez-Escalante expedition camped in the area in 1776. In fact, vega is the Spanish word for meadow. Follow the self-guided nature trail through the subalpine terrain, stopping at the interpretive stations along the way. Deer, elk, waterfowl, and wild turkey may be spotted in the area, as well as hawks and grouse.

Corn Lake Trail

Maps: Grand Valley Natural Resources and Tourism Council:
Biking Guide to the Grand Valley
Location: 10 miles from the Grand Junction Visitor Center.
Elevation Range: 4,650—4,650 feet
Length of Hike (round trip): 3 miles
Difficulty Rating: Easy
Seasons to Hike: All seasons
Special Features: Fishing; riparian habitat
Services: Restrooms and drinking water available at the trailhead
Managing Agencies: Riverfront Commission; Grand Junction
Parks; Colorado State Parks

Access: From the Visitor Center, travel east on Interstate 70 toward Glenwood Springs. Within 5.5 miles, take the Clifton/Delta exit (Exit 37). Travel in a southwesterly direction along I-70 Business Loop for 1.5 miles. Turn left onto Highway 141 heading south. Travel along Highway 141 for almost 2.5 miles. Park at the State Park Offices on the right side of the road before you cross the Colorado River.

Trail Description: Follow the trail as it runs west and parallel to the Colorado River and connects with the Colorado River Wildlife Area.

Palisade Trail

Maps: Grand Valley Natural Resources and Tourism Council:
        Biking Guide to the Grand Valley
Location: 12 miles from the Grand Junction Visitor Center
Elevation Range: 4,700—4,700 feet
Length of Hike (round trip): 0.75 mile
Difficulty Rating: Easy
Seasons to Hike: All seasons
Special Features: Scenic views
Services: None
Managing Agencies: Riverfront Commission; Grand Junction
        Parks; Colorado State Parks

Access: From the Visitor Center, travel east on Interstate 70 toward Glenwood Springs. Within 11 miles, take the Palisade exit (Exit 42) and turn right at the stop sign. Follow Alberts Avenue for 1 mile to the intersection with Highway 6. Turn left onto Highway 6 and travel eastward for 0.5 mile. Turn right on Brentwood Drive. Within 0.5 mile you will come to the trailhead parking lot.

Trail Description: The trailhead is located at the south end of Bentwood Drive. Follow the trail as it crosses the Grand Valley Irrigation Canal. The trail continues westward along the Colorado River. Enjoy the outstanding views of Mt. Garfield, Mt. Lincoln, the Grand Mesa, and the orchards and vineyards of Palisade and East Orchard Mesa.

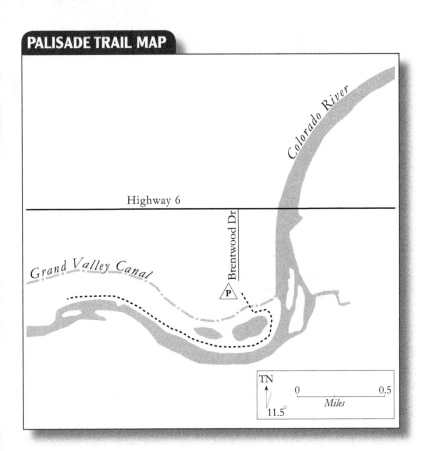

PALISADE TRAIL MAP

Colorado River

Highway 6

Brentwood Dr

Grand Valley Canal

P

TN
11.5°

0   Miles   0.5

Redlands Loop
(Audubon Trail, Connected Lakes Trail & Blue Heron Trail) ***

Maps: Grand Valley Natural Resources and Tourism Council:
    Biking Guide to the Grand Valley
Location: 4.5 miles from the Grand Junction Visitor Center
Elevation Range: 4,580—4,580 feet
Length of Hike (round trip): Varies
Difficulty Rating: Easy
Seasons to Hike: All seasons
Special Features: Lush, riparian habitat; wildlife
Services: Restrooms and picnic areas at various spots along the
    trails
Managing Agencies: Riverfront Commission; Grand Junction
    Parks; Colorado State Parks

REDLANDS LOOP TRAIL MAP

Redlands Parkway

Colorado River

River Road

South Rim Dr

23 Road

E. Road

Vista Grande Dr

Lake Road

Redlands Canal

Audubon Trail

Broadway - Highway 340

TN

11.5°

0   0.5
Miles

Access: From the Visitor Center, turn left (southwest) on Horizon Drive. At the roundabout, continue traveling southwest. Follow the signs for the Colorado National Monument by turning left (south) onto 7th Street, and then right (west) onto Grand Avenue. Pass through a major intersection with Highways 6 and 50 and cross the Colorado River. Grand Avenue is now Highway 340. Drive through the intersection with Monument Road. Pull into the parking area for Albertson's Shopping Center.

Trail Description: The Redlands Loop consists of three Colorado Riverfront Trails—Audubon Trail, Blue Heron Trail, and Connected Lakes Trail. The trailhead for the Audubon Trail is located at the west end of the shopping center. The trail is about 1.5 miles long and joins the Connected Lakes Trail. The Connected Lakes Trail runs parallel to the Redlands Canal and passes through the Connected Lakes State Park and a network of trails for 1 mile until it reaches Promontory Point. The Blue Heron Trail is located east of the shopping center and on the north side of the Colorado River. The trail runs parallel to the Colorado River; at 2.5 miles, it reaches the Redlands Parkway.

Watson Island/Old Mill Bridge Trails **

Maps: Grand Valley Natural Resources and Tourism Council:
Biking Guide to the Grand Valley
Location: 4.5 miles from the Grand Junction Visitor Center
Elevation Range: 4,580—4,580 feet
Length of Hike (round trip): Two short loops and a 1-mile loop
around Watson Island
Difficulty Rating: Easy
Seasons to Hike: All seasons
Special Features: Lush riparian habitat
Services: Restrooms and water available at the Botanical Gardens
Managing Agencies: Riverfront Commission; Grand Junction
Parks; Colorado State Parks

Access: From the Visitor Center, turn left (southwest) onto
Horizon Drive. At the roundabout, continue traveling southwest.
Follow the signs for the Colorado National Monument by turning
left (south) onto 7th Street. Continue along 7th Street for 3 miles

to the Botanical Gardens. Park in the Botanical Gardens parking area.

Trail Description: Watson Island, formerly a dumping site for all sorts of trash and waste, now stands as a wonderful example of what can happen when people unite to rectify environmental abuses of the past. Watson Island is indeed an island in the Colorado River. Two short paved loops are provided for hikers.

CHAPTER 6

Hiking on Grand Mesa

Grand Mesa

The Grand Mesa reminds me of my childhood stomping grounds of northern Wisconsin—mountainous terrain densely vegetated with lodgepole pines and numerous lakes (mosquitoes included). Although most large bodies of water in Colorado are not lakes but artificially created reservoirs, the Grand Mesa offers numerous natural lakes.

Geologically, the Grand Mesa is not a mesa; it is the world's largest flattop mountain. The Crag Crest Trail gives hikers stellar views of the San Juan Mountains to the south and is the premier hike on this flattop mountain.

Summer is the best hiking season. At the higher elevations, patches of columbine and other high-altitude flowers delight hikers; the lower elevations teem with wild roses. In addition, wildlife is abundant on the Grand Mesa. Large deer and elk herds abound, and the mesa is also home to a healthy black bear population. Fall is an ideal time for hikers to experience the gold and red of the changing aspens and scrub oaks. Backpacking opportunities abound in this area. Backpackers often combine fishing in remote lakes with their hiking.

Coal Creek Basin & Switchbacks Trail

Maps: USFS Grand Mesa map; USFS Grand Mesa Recreation Trails map; Trails Illustrated Grand Mesa topo map
Elevation Range: 6,100—10,000 feet
Location: 29 miles from the Grand Junction Visitor Center
Length of Hike (round trip): 12 miles. A recommended hike described below is 4.5 miles round trip.
Difficulty Rating: Difficult if the entire trail is hiked, otherwise moderate
Seasons to Hike: Summer, fall
Special Features: Varied terrain and vegetation; views
Services: None
Managing Agency: U.S. Forest Service: Grand Valley Ranger District, Mesa Lakes Ranger Station

Access: From the Visitor Center, turn left (southwest) onto Horizon Drive. At the roundabout, continue traveling southwest. Turn left (south) onto 7th Street, then right onto Ute Avenue. Turn left (south) onto 5th Street, which eventually turns into Highway 50. Cross the 5th Street Bridge and drive southeast toward Delta on Highway 50. Continue for approximately 8 miles to Whitewater. Travel 5.7 miles to the Lands End/Kannah Creek Road. Turn left and travel 3 miles; turn right onto Kannah Creek Road. Take another right immediately, staying on Kannah Creek Road. Continue for 7.3 miles, cross a cattle guard, and continue for 0.2 mile to a pull-out on the right side of the road; here you will see a "no camping" sign. The trailhead is 100 feet (south) back down the road.

Trail Description: The recommended hike of 4.5 miles round trip has an elevation gain of approximately 1,000 feet and takes you to the picturesque bridge at the Coal Creek Crossing. Begin hiking through piñon-juniper and sage country over a well-marked trail.

If you choose to continue beyond the bridge, the path eventually passes through meadows marked by patches of oakbrush and aspen; however, the trail is masked by overgrown vegetation through the meadows and is hard to follow. The upper reaches of the trail consist of steep switchbacks through aspen groves, pine trees, and boulder fields. The trail leads hikers to Lands End Road.

Alternative Access and Route from Lands End Road: Note that Lands End Road is maintained from June 1 through October 15. From the Lands End/Kannah Creek Road, travel 3 miles and turn left onto Lands End Road. Continue for almost 19 miles to the rim, bearing right at the "Y." Travel 3.5 miles and park at the pull-out on the right (near a cattle guard). Follow the trail marker down through the gate and descend 1 mile and 1,000 feet down the switchbacks.

Alternative Access and Route from the Grand Mesa: From the Grand Junction Visitor Center, take I-70 east for 17.3 miles to Exit 49 (Highway 65/Grand Mesa Scenic Byway). Drive approximately 31 miles to Lands End Road and turn right (west.) Drive 1.3 miles and bear right at the "Y." Continue for 8.5 miles to the switchback trailhead.

Coal Creek Trail

Maps: USFS Grand Mesa map; USFS Grand Mesa Recreation Trails map; Trails Illustrated Grand Mesa topo map
Elevation Range: 8,400—9,900 feet
Location: 35 miles from the Grand Junction Visitor Center
Length of Hike (round trip): Varies. The entire length is 18.5 miles round trip.
Difficulty Rating: Difficult if the entire trail is hiked. The shorter hikes are easy.
Seasons to Hike: Summer, fall
Special Features: Scenic views
Services: None
Managing Agency: U.S. Forest Service: Grand Valley Ranger District, Mesa Lakes Ranger Station

Access: From the Visitor Center, turn left (southwest) onto Horizon Drive. At the roundabout, continue traveling southwest. Turn left (south) onto 7th Street, then right onto Ute Avenue. Turn left (south) onto 5th Street, which eventually turns into Highway 50. Cross the 5th Street Bridge and drive southeast toward Delta on Highway 50. Continue for approximately 8 miles to Whitewater. Travel 5.7 miles to the Lands End/Kannah Creek Road. Turn left and travel 3 miles. Turn left onto Lands End Road. Continue for approximately 13.5 miles and turn right at a sign indicating the Wild Rose Picnic Ground. Continue for 0.1 mile to the parking area. The trailhead is to the south.

Trail Description: The trailhead is situated next to a picnic area surrounded by thick vegetation consisting of scrub oak and aspen. The trail leads first through the scrub oak and then through sub-alpine spruce and fir as it contours beneath the rim of the Grand Mesa. The upper meadows provide wide open views and a lush variety of wildflowers. The trail leads to Carson Lake.

Alternative Access from Lands End Road: Note that Lands End Road is maintained from June 1 through October 15. From the Lands End/Kannah Creek Road, travel 3 miles and turn left onto Lands End Road. Continue for almost 19 miles to the rim (passing the Wild Rose Campground). Bear right at the "Y." Travel 8.5 miles and turn right, following the sign for Carson Lake. Drive 1.6 miles to the parking area. The well-marked Coal Creek trail is next to the parking area.

Alternative Access from the Grand Mesa: The Coal Creek Trail may be accessed from Carson Lake. From the Grand Junction Visitor Center, take I-70 east for 17.3 miles to Exit 49 (Highway 65/Grand Mesa Scenic Byway). Drive approximately 31 miles to Lands End Road and turn right (west.) Drive 1.3 miles and bear left at the "Y. "Continue for 1.6 miles to Carson Lake.

Deep Creek/ Farmers Trail

Maps: USFS Grand Mesa map; USFS Grand Mesa Recreation Trails map; Trails Illustrated Grand Mesa topo map

Elevation Range: 8,300—10,200 feet
Location: 29 miles from the Grand Junction Visitor Center
Length of Hike (round trip): 6 miles
Difficulty Rating: Moderate
Seasons to Hike: Summer, fall
Special Features: Scenic views
Services: None
Managing Agency: U.S. Forest Service: Grand Valley Ranger
District, Mesa Lakes Ranger Station

Access: From the Grand Junction Visitor Center, take I-70 east for 17.3 miles to Exit 49 (Highway 65/Grand Mesa Scenic Byway). Drive approximately 31 miles to Lands End Road and turn right (west.) Drive 1.3 miles and bear right at the "Y." Continue for 5.4 miles to the Deep Creek Trail. Park on the right; the trailhead is on the left (south.)

Trail Description: Deep Creek Trail was a stockmen's trail used to connect the higher elevation cow camps to the lower range and ranch property. The trail initially runs parallel to the road. Trail marker posts identify the path through the thick meadow. The trail soon descends from the rim of the Grand Mesa through aspen and spruce-fir. Within 1 mile, hikers will reach the junction with Coal Creek Trail. This is the terminus of Deep Creek and the beginning of Farmers Trail. At this junction, hike west for about 0.25 mile. Turn left and follow the Farmers Trail marker. The Farmers Trail was a livestock trail connecting Coal Creek Trail with Kannah Creek Trail. Be sure to avoid the faint stock paths, especially when you reach a large meadow. Cross the meadow and look for the trail on the left side. The trail officially ends after it crosses Kannah Creek and reaches Kannah Creek Trail.

Indian Point Trail

Maps: USFS Grand Mesa map; USFS Grand Mesa Recreation
Trails map; Trails Illustrated Grand Mesa topo map
Location: 29 miles from the Grand Junction Visitor Center
Elevation Range: 6,100—10,000 feet
Length of Hike (round trip): 15 miles

Hiking the Indian Point Trail

Difficulty Rating: Difficult
Seasons to Hike: Summer, fall
Special Features: Scenic views
Services: None
Managing Agency: U.S. Forest Service: Grand Valley Ranger
District, Mesa Lakes Ranger Station

Access: From the Visitor Center, turn left (southwest) onto Horizon Drive. At the roundabout, continue traveling southwest. Turn left (south) onto 7th Street, then right onto Ute Avenue. Turn left (south) onto 5th Street, which eventually turns into Highway 50. Cross the 5th Street Bridge and drive southeast toward Delta on Highway 50. Continue for approximately 8 miles to Whitewater. Travel 5.7 miles to the Lands End/Kannah Creek Road. Turn left (east) and travel 3 miles. Turn right onto Kannah Creek Road. Take another right immediately, staying on Kannah Creek Road. Continue up the road for 7.3 miles and pull into a parking area immediately before crossing a cattle guard.

Trail Description: Begin at the Kannah Creek trailhead, but abandon it shortly for the Spring Camp Trail. Ascend the steep trail, which leads through piñon-juniper and sage country. As you gain elevation, you will travel through several ecosystems. The views open up along the oakbrush and through stands of aspen. Take the Indian Point Cutoff Trail, turning right. From this point, the trail is identified by trail marker posts. It is important to follow these markers, as range cattle have created paths of their own. Shortly after starting up the Indian Point Cutoff Trail, turn right (west) at an unmarked intersection next to a small creek. Cross the creek and head for a trail marker post in the middle of a meadow. Hike across the lush, colorful meadows to the intersection with the Indian Point Stock Drive Trail. Turn left (southeast) and follow the historic stock trail to the summit of Indian Point.

Spring Camp Trail To Blue Lake **

Maps: USFS Grand Mesa map; USFS Grand Mesa Recreation Trails map; Trails Illustrated Grand Mesa topo map
Location: 29 miles from the Grand Junction Visitor Center
Elevation Range: 6,100—9,000 feet
Length of Hike (round trip): 10 miles
Difficulty Rating: Difficult due to steep terrain and elevation gain
Seasons to Hike: Summer, fall
Special Features: Varied terrain and vegetation, scenic lake, fishing
Services: None
Managing Agency: U.S. Forest Service: Grand Valley Ranger District, Mesa Lakes Ranger Station

Access: From the Visitor Center, turn left (southwest) onto Horizon Drive. At the roundabout, continue traveling southwest. Turn left (south) onto 7th Street, then right onto Ute Avenue. Turn left (south) onto 5th Street, which eventually turns into Highway 50. Cross the 5th Street Bridge and drive southeast toward Delta on Highway 50. Continue for approximately 8 miles to Whitewater. Travel 5.7 miles to the Lands End/Kannah Creek Road. Travel 3 miles and turn right onto Kannah Creek Road. Take another right immediately, staying on Kannah Creek Road. Continue for 7.3 miles and pull into a parking area immediately before crossing a cattle guard.

Trail Description: This trail is an old pioneer trail used today by stockmen to move their stock down from high summer pastures. Begin at the Kannah Creek trailhead, but abandon it shortly thereafter for the Spring Camp Trail. Ascend the steep trail, which takes you through piñon-juniper and sage country. As you gain elevation, you will travel through several ecosystems. The views open along the oakbrush. Wildflowers—among them phlox, aster, penstemon, wild iris, and lupine—flourish during the summer. The hike is perfumed with the scent of wild roses as you pass through stands of aspen. When you reach the Indian Point Cutoff sign, stay left on the Spring Camp Trail. Within 0.5 mile, a sign indicates that Blue Lake is 1 mile farther along the trail. Continue on the trail to the lake.

Kannah Creek Trail *

Maps: USFS Grand Mesa map; USFS Grand Mesa Recreation Trails map; Trails Illustrated Grand Mesa topo map
Location: 29 miles from the Grand Junction Visitor Center
Elevation Range: 6,100—9,900 feet
Length of Hike (round trip): Varies. The entire length to Carson Lake is 24 miles round trip.
Difficulty Rating: Difficult if the entire trail is hiked. The shorter hikes are moderate.
Seasons to Hike: Summer, fall
Special Features: Varied terrain and vegetation; scenic lake
Services: None
Managing Agency: U.S. Forest Service: Grand Valley Ranger District, Mesa Lakes Ranger Station

Access: From the Visitor Center, turn left (southwest) onto Horizon Drive. At the roundabout, continue traveling southwest. Turn left (south) onto 7th Street, then right onto Ute Avenue. Turn left (south) onto 5th Street, which eventually turns into Highway 50. Cross the 5th Street Bridge and drive southeast toward Delta on Highway 50. Continue for approximately 8 miles to Whitewater. Travel 5.7 miles to the Lands End/Kannah Creek Road. Turn left (east) and travel three miles. Turn right onto Kannah Creek Road. Take another right immediately, staying on Kannah Creek Road.

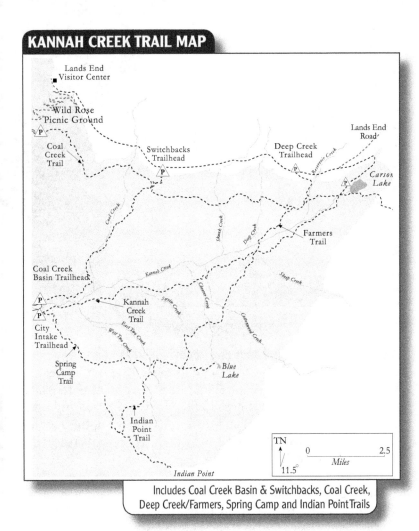

KANNAH CREEK TRAIL MAP

Lands End
Visitor Center

Wild Rose
Picnic Ground

P

Coal
Creek
Trail

Switchbacks
Trailhead

P

Lands End
Road

Deep Creek
Trailhead

P

Reservoir Creek

Carson
Lake

P

Coal Creek

Skunk Creek

Deep Creek

Farmers
Trail

Coal Creek
Basin Trailhead

Kannah Creek

Sheep Creek

P

P

City
Intake
Trailhead

Kannah
Creek
Trail

Sartin Creek

Cliff Creek

Cottonwood Creek

West Tine Creek

East Tine Creek

Spring
Camp
Trail

Blue
Lake

Indian
Point
Trail

TN

0   2.5
Miles

11.5°

Indian Point

Includes Coal Creek Basin & Switchbacks, Coal Creek,
Deep Creek/Farmers, Spring Camp and Indian Point Trails

Continue for 7.3 miles and pull into a parking area immediately
before crossing a cattle guard.

Trail Description: This trail may have been used by the Ute Indians
as a hunting route and to gain access to the Grand Mesa. Begin
at the Kannah Creek trailhead and hike along Kannah Creek
through piñon-juniper and sage country. As you gain elevation,
the trail leads through sub-alpine meadows and stands of spruce
and fir. The trail ends at Carson Lake, which is also accessible by
vehicle from the Grand Mesa Scenic Byway.

Hiking the Cottonwood Trail

Alternative Access from Lands End Road: Note that Lands End Road is maintained from June 1 through October 15. From the Lands End/Kannah Creek Road, travel 3 miles and turn left onto Lands End Road. Continue for almost 19 miles to the rim, bearing right at the "Y." Travel 8.5 miles and turn right, following the sign for Carson Lake. Drive 1.6 miles to the parking area. To reach the Kannah Creek trailhead, cross the reservoir levi.

Alternative Access from the Grand Mesa: The Kannah Creek Trail may be accessed from Carson Lake. From the Grand Junction Visitor Center, take I-70 east for 17.3 miles to Exit 49 (Highway 65/Grand Mesa Scenic Byway). Drive approximately 31 miles to Lands End Road and turn right (west.) Drive 1.3 miles and bear left at the "Y." Continue for 1.6 miles to Carson Lake.

Rapid Creek Trail

Maps: USGS 7.5 minute map: Palisade, Cameo
Location: 17 miles from the Grand Junction Visitor Center
Elevation Range: 5,300—7,000 feet
Length of Hike (round trip): Varies, 2 to 10 miles

RAPID CREEK TRAIL MAP

Difficulty Rating: Easy
Seasons to Hike: All seasons
Special Features: Year-round stream
Services: None
Managing Agency: U.S. Forest Service: Grand Valley Ranger
District, Mesa Lakes Ranger Station

Access: Travel east on Interstate 70 toward Glenwood Springs.
Within 11 miles, take the Palisade exit (Exit 42) and turn right at
the stop sign. Follow Alberta Avenue for 1 mile to the intersection
of Highway 6. Turn left on Highway 6 and travel eastward for 2
miles. Turn right on Rapid Creek Road. In less than 1 mile, the
road will turn to gravel; veer right and continue for 1 mile to the
trailhead parking lot.

Trail Description: From the parking area, pass through the gate.
Travel east on the abandoned jeep trail. The trail parallels the
Rapid Creek, and after a mile or so, a hiking option exits to the
right (south). This trail turns into another abandoned jeep trail

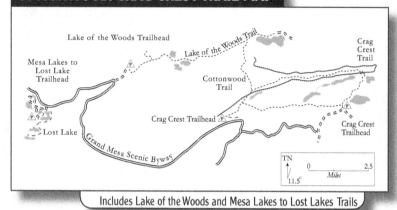

and continues up another drainage. Hikers can pursue the Rapid Creek Trail to the top of the Grand Mesa.

Cottonwood Trail

Maps: USFS Grand Mesa map; USFS Grand Mesa Recreation Trails map; Trails Illustrated Grand Mesa topo map
Location: 50 miles from the Grand Junction Visitor Center
Elevation Range: 10,380—10,800 feet
Length of Hike (round trip): 6 miles round trip to Cottonwood Lake
Difficulty Rating: Moderate
Seasons to Hike: Summer, fall
Special Features: Scenic lake
Services: Year-round lodging on the Grand Mesa
Managing Agency: U.S. Forest Service: Grand Valley Ranger District, Mesa lakes Ranger Station

Access: From the Grand Junction Visitor Center, take I-70 east for 17.3 miles to Exit 49 (Highway 65/Grand Mesa Scenic Byway). Drive approximately 33 miles to the West Crag Crest trailhead parking area.

Trail Description: Hike northeast along the trail for 0.5 mile to the intersection with the Lower Loop Trail. At the sign, stay left and

Hiking the Crag Crest Trail

follow the signs for Cottonwood Trail, which is another mile of hiking up a steady grade. The next junction is with the two trails leading to the Crag Crest East trailhead, via either the Lower Loop or the Crest. Continue left, picking up the Cottonwood Trail for 1.5 miles to Cottonwood Lake. The trail meanders through some lush meadows filled with grasses and wildflowers before descending through aspen and spruce-fir terrain. Shortly before reaching Cottonwood Lake, the trail intersects with the Lake of the Woods Trail. The lake rewards hikers with beautiful views, including a backdrop of Crag Crest along the south side of the lake.

Crag Crest ***

Maps: USFS Grand Mesa map; USFS Grand Mesa Recreation
Trails map; Trails Illustrated Grand Mesa topo map
Location: 50 miles from the Grand Junction Visitor Center
Elevation Range: 10,150—11,190 feet
Length of Hike (round trip): 10 miles

Difficulty Rating: Strenuous
Seasons to Hike: Summer, early fall
Special Features: Scenic vistas, geological history
Services: Restrooms at trailheads
Managing Agency: U.S. Forest Service: Grand Valley Ranger
District, Mesa Lakes Ranger Station

Access: From the Grand Junction Visitor Center, take I-70 east for 17.3 miles to Exit 49 (Highway 65/Grand Mesa Scenic Byway). Drive approximately 33 miles to the West Crag Crest trailhead parking area.

Trail Description: Hike northeast along the trail for 0.5 mile to the intersection with the Lower Loop Trail. At the sign, stay left and follow the signs for Crag Crest Trail. The next junction is with the two trails leading to the Crag Crest East trailhead via either the Lower Loop or the Crest. Continue toward the Crest. On the Crest portion of the trail, sections of the ridge are narrow and have steep drop-offs. While at a high point, enjoy 360-degree views of the Bookcliffs to the northwest, the Elk Mountains to the east, the West Elk Mountains and the San Juan Range to the south, and the La Sal Mountains and Uncompahgre Plateau to the west. Descend 1,000 feet through open meadows and stands of spruce, sub-alpine fir, and quaking aspen to Eggleston Lake and the East trailhead. Continue westward on the Lower Loop toward the West trailhead.

Alternative Access and Route: To reach the East trailhead, continue along the Grand Mesa Scenic Byway past the West trailhead. As the highway curves southeast along Island Lake, turn left at the Visitor Center and follow the road northeast past Alexander Lake. At Eggleston Lake, look for the trailhead on the other side of the road.

Lake of the Woods Trail *

Maps: USFS Grand Mesa map; USFS Grand Mesa Recreation
Trails map; Trails Illustrated Grand Mesa topo map
Location: 50 miles from the Grand Junction Visitor Center

Hiking the Lake of the Woods Trail

Elevation Range: 10,000—10,200 feet
Length of Hike (round trip): 13 miles round trip to Cottonwood
    Lake
Difficulty Rating: Moderate
Seasons to Hike: Summer, fall
Special Features: Scenic lakes
Services: Year round lodging on the Grand Mesa
Managing Agency: U.S. Forest Service: Grand Valley Ranger
    District, Mesa Lakes Ranger Station

Access: From the Grand Junction Visitor Center, take I-70 east
for 17.3 miles to Exit 49 (Highway 65/Grand Mesa Scenic Byway).
Drive approximately 28.5 miles to a hairpin curve and turn left
onto 250 Road. Travel 0.4 mile to the parking area.

Trail Description: Follow this easy trail through open meadows,
marshes, and stands of aspen and spruce-fir trees. The Bull
Creek Reservoirs are pretty places to have a picnic or go fishing.
Cottonwood Lake rewards hikers with beautiful views, including a
backdrop of Crag Crest along the south side of the lake.

Mesa Lakes to Lost Lake

Maps: USFS Grand Mesa map; USFS Grand Mesa Recreation
Trails map; Trails Illustrated Grand Mesa topo map
Location: 43 miles from the Grand Junction Visitor Center and
continue for another mile or so to Glacier Springs Picnic
Area.
Elevation Range: 9,900—10,200 feet
Length of Hike (round trip): 2.5 miles
Difficulty Rating: Easy
Seasons to Hike: Summer, fall
Special Features: Scenic lakes
Services: Year-round lodging on the Grand Mesa
Managing Agency: U.S. Forest Service: Grand Valley Ranger
District, Mesa Lakes Ranger Station

Access: From the Grand Junction Visitor Center, take I-70 east
for 17.3 miles to Exit 49 (Highway 65/Grand Mesa Scenic Byway).
Drive approximately 24.5 miles to the Mesa Lakes turnoff. Drive
into the Mesa Lakes Resort and continue toward Sunset Lake. At
Sunset Lake, turn left (southeast)

Trail Description: Head south around Mesa Lake. At the Deep Creek
Trail cutoff, stay left on the Mesa Lake Shoreline Trail. Within
minutes, follow the Lost Lake Trail by heading right at a fork in
the trail. Go left at the junction with Trail 502. The trail skirts
around South Mesa Lake and a short switchback trail leads hikers
to Lost Lake.

CHAPTER 7

McDonald Creek Canyon Petroglyphs

Rabbit Valley

The westernmost area described in this guide, Rabbit Valley is only a few miles from the Utah border. Rabbit Valley is also part of the recently established Colorado Canyons National conservation Area. This section of the NCA is located on the north side of the Colorado River. Most who recreate here are motorized users and mountain bikers but the region offers a few hikes, and each is distinctly different. The Trail Through Time is an interesting and unique hike because dinosaur fossils are featured along the trail in conjunction with interpretive markers. The Rabbit's Ear Trail is a steep hike through piñon-juniper and scrub oak country. The trail summits a ridge with striking views of the Colorado River below and the La Sal Mountains in the distance. McDonald Canyon is one of few locations where visitors can see Fremont Indian rock art. The Fremont Indians were a small tribe of Native Americans that inhabited this land 10,000 years ago. The canyon is scenic, and so is the short drive leading hikers there. Rabbit Valley also provides choice nonfee camping locations.

Hiking in McDonald Creek Canyon

The predominant Indian tribe of the Grand Valley and western Colorado was the Ute. Primarily a sheep herding tribe, the Utes were lead by the famous Chief Ouray. Chief Ouray was a highly intelligent man who spoke three languages: Ute, Spanish, and English. Chief Ouray strongly advocated nonaggressive interactions with the white settlers. He realized early on that raging war against the white man would be futile and would lead only to the annihilation of his own people. In the end, because of Chief Ouray's statesmanship and leadership skills, the Utes suffered far fewer atrocities than other tribes during that unfortunate era. Today, there are several Ute Indian settlements in southwestern Colorado and Utah.

McDonald Creek Canyon Trail**

Maps: BLM McDonald Creek Cultural Resource Area map; USGS 7.5 minute map: Bitter Creek Well
Location: 33 miles from the Grand Junction Visitor Center
Elevation Range: 4,350—4,450 feet
Length of Hike (round trip): 4 miles
Difficulty Rating: Moderate

McDONALD CREEK CANYON TRAIL MAP

Rabbit's Ear Trailhead
To Denver
Trail Through Time Trailhead
McDonald Creek
McDonald Creek Canyon Trailhead
Colorado River
TN
11.5°
0
0.5
Miles

Includes Rabbit's Ear and Trail Through Time Trails

Seasons to Hike: Spring, fall, winter
Special Features: Rock art, scenic canyon
Services: Restrooms at the trailhead.
Managing Agency: Bureau of Land Management: Grand Junction Resource Area

Access: Travel west on Interstate 70 from Grand Junction approximately 30 miles. Follow signs for Dinosaur Quarry Trail and Rabbit Valley 1/2 Mile by taking Exit 2. Turn left (south) at the stop sign and cross the freeway on the overpass. The road turns to gravel almost immediately. Within 0.5 mile, cross a cattle guard and take the road straight ahead. A high-clearance vehicle is necessary because visitors will encounter a couple of steep, rocky sections and a stream crossing. Depending on the weather, there may be loose sand or mud. Follow the road for about 2.5 miles to a monolith—Castle Rock—on the right side of the road, as well as a small parking area and visitor information sign. Pass the rock and turn left into a parking area.

Trail Description: McDonald Creek Canyon is a classic desert oasis featuring huge sandstone undercuts and an intermittent stream flanked by lush habitat that includes cottonwoods, pigweed, and serviceberry bushes. Hikers will enjoy searching for the area's pictographs and petroglyphs. The canyon opens into Ruby Canyon on the Colorado River. Across the river and a little downstream is the mouth of Knowles Canyon.

Alternative Access and Route: A trail runs along the west rim of McDonald Canyon and provides great views. To access this trail, when you reach the large rock, continue straight ahead instead of turning left to reach the parking area for the McDonald Creek Canyon Trail. Travel along this road for approximately 2 miles. Do not cross the cattle guard, but turn left into a beautiful picnic area. Look for the trailhead sign. This trail will take you down to the rim overlooking Ruby Canyon. The trail runs eastbound until it reaches the rim of McDonald Creek; at that point, it leads upstream (north).

Rabbit's Ear Trail *

Maps: USGS 7.5 minute map: Ruby Canyon; Bitter Creek Well
Location: 35 miles from the Grand Junction Visitor Center
Elevation Range: 5,000—5,780 feet
Length of Hike (round trip): 5 miles
Difficulty Rating: Moderate
Seasons to Hike: Spring, fall, and winter
Services: Restrooms at the trailhead
Special Features: Panoramic views at Ruby Canyon Overlook of the La Sal Mountains, the Book Cliffs, and the Grand Mesa

Hiking the Rabbit's Ear Trail

Managing Agency: Bureau of Land Management: Grand Junction
  Resource Area

Access: Travel west on Interstate 70 from Grand Junction for
approximately 30 miles. Follow signs for "Dinosaur Quarry Trail"
and "Rabbit Valley 1/2 Mile" by taking Exit 2. Turn left (south)
at the stop sign and cross the freeway on the overpass. The road
turns to gravel almost immediately. Within 0.5 mile, cross a cattle
guard and veer left (east). This is the Kokopelli Trail, a mountain
bike trail winding 142 miles to link Grand Junction to Moab.
Follow the Kokopelli Trail, which is a well-maintained gravel road
at this point running parallel to I-70. Take this road for about 4.5
miles, passing an old stock corral to the south. Park in the small
area by the BLM trailhead sign for Rabbit's Ear trail.

Trail Description: This moderate trail through juniper and sage
country features 360 degree views. After about 1 mile of hiking
up a steady grade, pass through a sandstone slot. At this point
hikers can see the La Sal Mountains, as well as the Colorado River
below. Gain a little bit more elevation before reaching a plateau

and an easy finish to the Ruby Canyon Overlook of the Colorado River. From this vantage point, hikers can view the mouth of Mee Canyon.

Rabbit Valley BLM Trail Through Time ***

Maps: BLM and Museum of Western Colorado: Trail Though Time trail map; USGS 7.5 minute map: Bitter Creek Well
Location: 30 miles from the Grand Junction Visitor Center
Elevation Range: 4,600—4,700 feet
Length of Hike (round trip): 1.5 mile loop
Difficulty Rating: Moderate
Seasons to Hike: All seasons
Special Features: Fossils, quarry, geology, scenic views
Services: Restrooms are located beyond the parking area.
Managing Agencies: Bureau of Land Management: Grand Junction Resource Area; Museum of Western Colorado

Access: Travel west on Interstate 70 from Grand Junction approximately 30 miles. Follow signs for Dinosaur Quarry Trail and Rabbit Valley 1/2 Mile by taking Exit 2. Turn right (north) at the stop sign and park in the parking area.

Trail Description: The Rabbit Valley Research Natural Area and Trail Through Time takes hikers through an active dinosaur quarry that continues to be the site of significant fossil finds. Millions of years ago, this place was a lush land made up of forests, rivers, and swamps that served as home to herds of dinosaurs. The vegetation along this trail today consists of saltbush and juniper trees, prickly pear cactus and wild flowers. The interpretive trail allows hikers to see fossils in a natural setting, including the vertebrae of two different types of dinosaur—the Diplodocus and the Camarasaurus. Be sure to stop at the overlook and take in the views the La Sal Mountains, Ruby Canyon on the Colorado River, and the Uncompahgre Plateau.

CHAPTER 8

Uncompahgre Plateau View

Uncompahgre Plateau & Basin

The Uncompahgre Plateau and Basin offer incredible diversity for the hiker. The area offers mountainous hikes through aspens and huge ponderosa pines, deep sandstone canyons, and a vertically foliated granite valley similar to Yosemite Valley in California.

Dominguez Canyon is the jewel of the area. The deep, pristine red sandstone canyon has a large population of bighorn sheep. The stream flowing through the canyon is set in the lower Precambrian layer of granite, offering oasis-like settings. Small waterfalls and deep plunge pools are common sights in this canyon. One can also find numerous examples of Native American rock art. Backpackers will find Dominguez Canyon ideal for multiple day backpacking trips.

Dominguez Canyon, as well as Escalante Canyon, were named after famous Catholic missionaries who traveled these lands.

Padre Dominguez, for example, established the Spanish Trail, which is now preserved for its historical significance. The trail is not listed in this chapter, but in the "Other Trails" section.

Although I live an easy drive from the Uncompahgre Plateau, I often find myself camping in various locations on the plateau simply because of the alluring solitude and beauty. Hikers will enjoy breathtaking views of the La Sal Mountains as they travel along the western regions of the plateau. The northern regions, including the Unaweep Trail, offer bird's-eye views of the rugged and vertical Unaweep Canyon. Fall hikers seeking out golden aspens will be well rewarded for their endeavors. The Uncompahgre Plateau also has the most concentrated black bear population in the state.

Lower Big Dominguez Canyon ***

Maps: Forest Service map: Uncompahgre National Forest; USGS 7.5 minute map: Dominguez, Triangle Mesa, Escalante Forks
Location: 30 from the Grand Junction Visitor Center
Elevation Range: 4,735—7,200 feet
Length of Hike (round trip): Varies; 2 miles to multi-day travel
Difficulty Rating: Moderate, except for steep descent into the canyon
Seasons to Hike: Spring, summer, and fall
Special Features: Desert bighorn sheep; pool drops; red rock canyon views; petroglyghs; solitude
Services: None
Managing Agency: Bureau of Land Management: Grand Junction Resource Area

Access: From the Visitor Center, turn left (southwest) onto Horizon Drive. At the roundabout, continue traveling southwest. Turn left (south) onto 7th Street, then right onto Ute Avenue. Turn left (south) on 5th Street, which eventually turns into Highway 50. Cross the 5th Street Bridge and drive southeast towards Delta on Highway 50. Continue for approximately 8 miles

To Parking

Gunnison River

Unaweep/
Tabeguache
Byway

To Cactus Park

Difficult 4WD

Divide Road

Big Dominguez Canyon

Little Dominguez Canyon

P

Dominquez
Campground

TN

0 — 2.5
Miles

11.5°

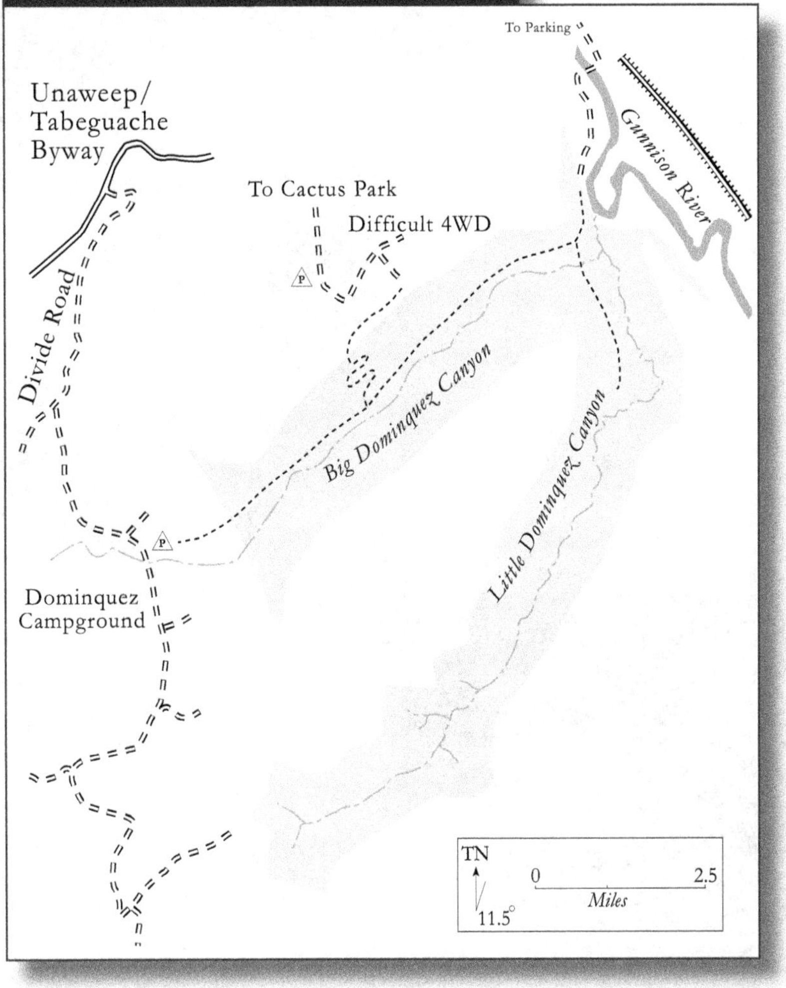

to Whitewater. Travel 0.5 mile to Highway 141 and turn right onto the Unaweep/Tabeguache Scenic and Historic Byway. Take this beautiful route towards Gateway for approximately 9 miles. Turn left at the sign indicating Cactus Park. Within 1 mile, you will reach a fork in this dirt road. Bear left. Travel 1.3 miles and at this fork, bear right. Travel 1.7 miles to the next fork. Turn right again and travel 0.2 mile to a road on the left marked by a sign for Dominguez Canyon Access. Follow this sign for 3 miles to the trailhead. A high-clearance vehicle is needed for the last mile before the trailhead.

Hiking in Big Dominguez Canyon

Trail Description: Follow the dirt road to the rim and look for the BLM trail sign on the right (southwest.) Hike southwest along the rim and up the canyon. Keep an eye out for the desert sheep along this northern rim. Pass a BLM sign and slickrock wash. At the next BLM sign, follow the cairns while descending into the canyon. At the sign for Cactus Park, head down the canyon towards the Gunnison River. Enjoy the stirring canyon views, numerous plunge pools, petroglyphs on several large sandstone boulders, and lush cottonwoods as you approach the Gunnison River.

Alternative Access: From the Grand Junction Visitor Center, turn left (south) onto Horizon Drive. At the roundabout, go straight. Turn left (south) onto 7th Street, then right onto Ute Avenue. Turn left (south) onto 5th Street, which eventually turns into Highway 50. From the 5th Street Bridge, drive southeast towards Delta on Highway 50 for 20.5 miles to Bridgeport Road. Turn right on Bridgeport and travel for 3 miles to a parking area along the Gunnison River. Hike upstream along the railroad tracks or paralleling dirt road until you come to a bridge crossing the Gunnison River. Cross the bridge and hike upstream along an abandoned jeep trail to the mouth of Dominguez Canyon.

Boaters can access the mouth of the canyon without crossing private property. A popular trip involves a float down the Gunnison River, putting in at Escalante Canyon, and taking out at Bridgeport or Whitewater. From Escalante, a half-day float downriver will lead to the mouth of Dominguez Canyon, which is a popular and beautiful camping area. This section of the Gunnison River offers views of orchards and small ranching operations.

Upper Big Dominguez Canyon *

Maps: U.S. Forest Service: Uncompahgre National Forest map; USGS 7.5 minute map: Dominguez, Triangle Mesa, Escalante Forks
Location: 40 miles from the Grand Junction Visitor Center
Elevation Range: 4,735—7,200 feet
Length of Hike (round trip): Varies; 2 miles to multi-day travel
Difficulty Rating: Moderate
Seasons to Hike: Summer, fall
Special Features: Deep sandstone canyon; perennial stream
Services: Restrooms and camping area
Managing Agency: Bureau of Land Management: Grand Junction Resource Area

Access: From the Visitor Center, turn left (southwest) onto Horizon Drive. At the roundabout, continue traveling southwest. Turn left (south) onto 7th Street, then right onto Ute Avenue. Turn left (south) onto 5th Street, which eventually turns into Highway 50. Cross the 5th Street Bridge and drive southeast towards Delta on Highway 50. Continue for approximately 8 miles to Whitewater. Travel 0.5 mile to Highway 141 and turn right onto the Unaweep/Tabeguache Scenic and Historic Byway. Take this beautiful route towards Gateway for approximately 14.5 miles. Turn left at the sign for Divide Road. Travel up this steep gravel road for about 6 miles to the Dominguez Resource Conservation Area sign. Turn left here and continue for approximately 5 miles to the Dominguez trailhead and camp area.

Trail Description: A well-marked trail descends gradually through diverse vegetation, including ponderosa pine, Douglas fir, piñon-juniper, oakbrush, and cottonwood stands. Occasionally, the trail skirts the Big Dominguez Creek. As hikers descend in elevation, the views of the lower reaches of this delightful canyon unfold. Journey down the trail for approximately 4 miles to the Cactus Park sign. This is a good terminus for a day hike.

McCarty Trail

Maps: U.S. Forest Service: Uncompahgre National Forest map; USGS 7.5 minute map: Good Point
Location: 33 miles from the Grand Junction Visitor Center
Elevation Range: 5,500—7,300 feet
Length of Hike (round trip): 4 miles
Difficulty Rating: Moderate
Seasons to Hike: Spring, fall, and winter
Special Features: Sweeping views of the Elk Mountain Range and the West Elk Mountains
Services: None
Managing Agencies: Bureau of Land Management; Colorado Plateau Mountain Bike Trail Association

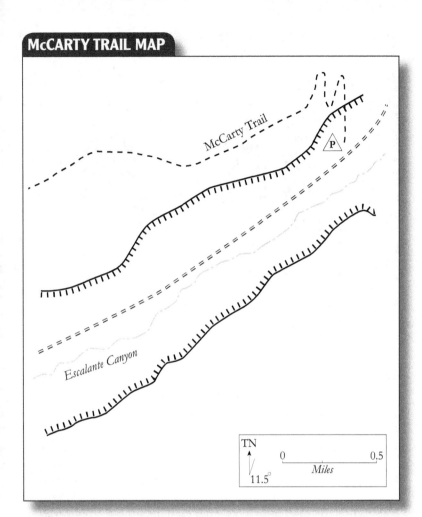

McCARTY TRAIL MAP

McCarty Trail

P

Escalante Canyon

TN
11.5°

0   Miles   0.5

Access: From the Visitor Center, turn left (southwest) onto Horizon Drive. At the roundabout, continue traveling southwest. Turn left (south) onto 7th Street, then right onto Ute Avenue. Turn left (south) onto 5th Street, which eventually turns into Highway 50. Cross the 5th Street Bridge and drive southeast towards Delta on Highway 50. Continue for approximately 8 miles to Whitewater. Travel 18 miles to the Escalante Canyon turnoff. Turn right and travel down the gravel road for roughly 4.7 miles and park in the pullout on the right. You will see a small BLM bicycle trail sign. This trail is a section of the Tabaguache mountain bike trail that is very suitable for hiking.

Escalante Canyon

Trail Description: This trail is a small section of the Tabeguache Trail, which is a 142-mile mountain bike trail connecting Montrose to Grand Junction. Tabeguache is a word that originated with the Spanish explorer Escalante and means "place where the snow melts first." This trail climbs steadily up an old dirt road. Soon the road turns to a trail as it continues up through piñon-juniper country to a dry grass meadow. Follow the trail northeast through the meadow until the trail climbs again and leads to the top of the mesa. At this point, hikers have traveled about 1.5 miles. To continue, follow the trail as it continues west on fairly easy terrain to pine forests.

Don't miss the historic cabins and petroglyphs that lie farther up the road along scenic Escalante Canyon. Walker Cabin was built in 1911 and constructed of stone and mud mortar. Later, the original mortar was covered in cement. Captain Smith's Cabin is farther up Escalante Canyon. The captain, wounded in the Civil War, moved to the canyon in 1907.

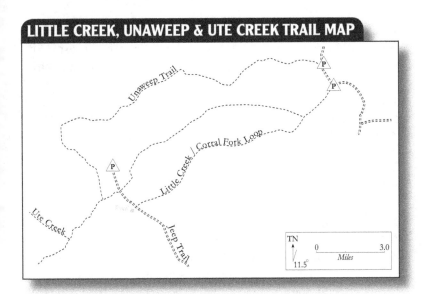

Little Creek/Corral Fork Loop **

Maps: U.S. Forest Service: Uncompahgre National Forest map,
    USGS 7.5 minute map: Castro Reservoir, Pine Mountain
Location: 44 miles from the Grand Junction Visitor Center
Elevation Range: 8,100—9,100 feet
Length of Hike (round trip): 10-mile loop
Difficulty Rating: Moderate
Seasons to Hike: Summer, fall
Special Features: Scenic drainages
Services: None
Managing Agency: U.S. Forest Service: Grand Valley Ranger
    District

Access: From the Visitor Center, turn left (south) onto Horizon
Drive. At the roundabout, go straight. Turn left (south) onto 7th
Street, then right onto Ute Avenue. Turn left (south) onto 5th
Street, which eventually turns into Highway 50. Cross the 5th
Street Bridge and drive southeast towards Delta on Highway 50.
Continue for approximately 8 miles to Whitewater. Travel 0.5 mile
to Highway 141 and turn right onto the Unaweep/Tabeguache
Scenic and Historic Byway. Take this beautiful route towards
Gateway. After approximately 13.5 miles, turn left onto Divide

Road. Travel up the switchbacks onto the plateau. Within about 6 miles, you will enter the Uncompahgre National Forest. Drive 3.5 miles and turn right at the Big Creek Reservoir turnoff. Drive along the dirt road for approximately 5 miles. Turn right at the "Y" junction and continue for approximately 1 mile. Park at the small pullout. The unmarked trailhead is on the southwest side of the road and on the northwest side of Little Creek.

Trail Description: The first 0.25 mile of the trail is an old off-road-vehicle route. The rest of the trail through the Little Creek and Corral Fork drainages consists of a small footpath. Cabin Trail, Rim Road, and Basin Trail are dirt roads. Follow the trail along the scenic Little Creek Drainage. Within 0.3 mile, you will reach a trailhead signpost for Corral Fork. Head left (southwest) and continue up the drainage for 3.5 miles through open, grassy meadows and stands of spruce and aspen. The trail intersects with the Cabin Trail (a 4WD road) at the top of the Uncompahgre Plateau. Head right (southwest) along the Cabin Trail for about 1 mile. Then head right (northwest) again when the trail meets Rim Road. Walk along the road for 1 mile, passing Big Pond on the left. Take the Basin Trail on your right (northeast) for about 0.25 mile until you see the Corral Fork Trail. Follow the Corral Fork Trail down the drainage for about 4 miles to its junction with Little Creek, and continue back to your vehicle.

Ute Creek Trail

Maps: U.S. Forest Service: Uncompahgre National Forest map;
USGS 7.5 minute map: Pine Mountain
Location: 51 miles from the Grand Junction Visitor Center
Elevation Range: 5,500—9,200 feet
Length of Hike (round trip): Varies; 4 to 10 miles
Difficulty Rating: Difficult—strenuous descent along Snowshoe
Trail
Seasons to Hike: Summer
Special Features: Impressive vistas
Managing Agency: U. S. Forest Service: Grand Valley Ranger
District

Access: From the Visitor Center, turn left (south) onto Horizon Drive. At the roundabout, go straight. Turn left (south) onto 7th Street, then right onto Ute Avenue. Turn left (south) onto 5th Street, which eventually turns into Highway 50. Cross the 5th Street Bridge and drive southeast towards Delta on Highway 50. Continue for approximately 8 miles to Whitewater. Travel 0.5 mile to Highway 141 and turn right onto the Unaweep/Tabeguache Scenic and Historic Byway. Take this beautiful route towards Gateway for approximately 14.5 miles. Turn left at the sign for Divide Road. Travel up this steep gravel road for about 6 miles to the Dominguez Resource Conservation Area sign. Continue straight ahead. Divide Road now enters forest service property, and is also known as Forest Service Road 402. Continue for 10 miles or so as you travel through stands of old-growth ponderosa pine and meadows marked by aspen groves. As you approach Divide Forks Campground, turn right on Uranium Road (Forest Service Road 404.) Within 3 miles, turn right onto Rim Trail. Drive for approximately 3 miles and pass through a stock gate. Turn left almost immediately at the first fork and left again 1 mile later at the second fork. Look for the Snowshoe Trail sign on the left and park.

Trail Description: The trailhead is situated at the top of the plateau, affording unrestricted views of the La Sal Mountains. Follow the trail as it drops abruptly through thick oakbrush into the Ute Creek drainage. When you approach a small opening lined by a fence running north-south, head south and pick up a dirt road. Cross through an electric fence as you continue to drop. Shortly after you reach an old cabin and barn, cross the drainage and continue for a few more minutes until you reach the Ute Creek trail on the north side. Follow the abandoned road downstream through the pine forest. When deciding when to turn back, don't forget the steep ascent you must tackle before you reach your car.

Unaweep Trail *

Maps: U.S. Forest Service: Uncompahgre National Forest map;
USGS 7.5 minute map: Casto Reservior, Pine Mountain

Location: 44 miles from the Grand Junction Visitor Center

Elevation Range: 8,300—8,800 feet

Length of Hike (round trip): Varies. The entire length of the trail is 16.5 miles one way; therefore a day hike is not sufficient to cover the entire trail

Difficulty Rating: Moderate

Seasons to Hike: Summer, fall

Special Features: The middle section of the trail offers scenic views overlooking Unaweep Canyon, and there are views of La Sal Mountains on the western part of the trail. The area is prime black bear habitat.

Services: None

Managing Agency: U.S. Forest Service: Grand Valley Ranger District

Access: From the Visitor Center, turn left (south) onto Horizon Drive. At the roundabout, go straight. Turn left (south) onto 7th Street, then right onto Ute Avenue. Turn left (south) onto 5th Street, which eventually turns into Highway 50. Cross the 5th Street Bridge and drive southeast towards Delta on Highway 50. Continue for approximately 8 miles to Whitewater. Travel 0.5 mile to Highway 141 and turn right onto the Unaweep/Tabeguache Scenic and Historic Byway. Take this beautiful route toward Gateway. After approximately 13.5 miles, turn left onto Divide Road. Travel up the switchbacks onto the plateau. Within about 6 miles, you will enter the Uncompahgre National Forest. Drive 3.5 miles and turn right at the Big Creek Reservoir turnoff. Drive along the dirt road for approximately 5 miles and turn right at the "Y" junction. Drive approximately 1 mile, passing Little Creek on the northwest side of the road. Continue for 0.3 mile up a steep dirt road and park at the intersection of Unaweep and Basin Trails. A high-clearance vehicle will be required for the last 0.3 mile.

Trail Description: The Unaweep Trail forks north off the Basin Trail and ascends into stands of aspen and spruce. Within a couple of miles, the trail levels out as hikers reach the plateau and a trail intersection. Continue northwest along the Unaweep Trail for about 50 yards. Little Bear Lake can be viewed on the right (north) side of the trail. After you pass the lake, look closely for a cairn and the continuation of the trail on the left (south) side. If you continue straight, you will reach a vista overlooking Unaweep Canyon, but this is a dead-end. Take the trail as it descends steeply into Bear Canyon. At the bottom of the drainage, the trail intersects with the Middle Fork Trail and then the North Fork Trail. After crossing North Fork, the trail skirts around the hillside overlooking Unaweep Canyon. From this point on, hikers are treated to outstanding views of the canyon along a fairly level trail.

Alternative Access and Route: Unaweep Trail may also be accessed from its southern end. Instead of turning off Divide Road at Big Creek Road, continue along Divide Road. As you approach Divide Forks Campground, turn right onto Uranium Road (Forest Service Road 404.) Within 3 miles, turn right onto Rim Trail. Drive for approximately 3 miles and pass through a stock gate. Turn left at the first fork and left again at the second fork. Look for the Snowshoe Trail sign on the left and park. Hike 0.3 mile down the steep upper Snowshoe Trail. At this point, the trail intersects with Unaweep Trail. Head right (northwest) along the trail as it skirts along the hillside, eventually overlooking Unaweep Canyon.

Upper Bench Trail

Maps: U.S. Forest Service: Uncompahgre National Forest map; USGS 7.5 minute map: Uncompahgre Butte, Snipe, Atkinson Creek
Location: 58 miles from the Grand Junction Visitor Center
Elevation Range: 8,900—8,900 feet
Length of Hike (round trip): 15 miles
Difficulty Rating: Moderate
Seasons to Hike: Summer, fall
Special Features: Dense pine and aspen forest
Services: None
Managing Agency: U.S. Forest Service: Grand Valley Ranger District

Access: From the Visitor Center, turn left (south) onto Horizon Drive. At the roundabout, go straight. Turn left (south) onto 7th Street, then right onto Ute Avenue. Turn left (south) onto 5th

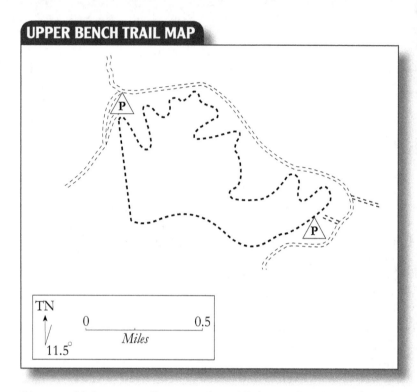

TN

0   0.5

Miles

11.5°

Street, which eventually turns into Highway 50. Cross the 5th Street Bridge and drive southeast toward Delta on Highway 50. Continue for approximately 8 miles to Whitewater. Travel 0.5 mile to Highway 141 and turn right onto the Unaweep/Tabeguache Scenic and Historic Byway. Take this beautiful route toward Gateway. After approximately 13.5 miles, turn left onto Divide Road. Travel up the switchbacks onto the plateau. Within about 6 miles, you will enter the Uncompahgre National Forest. Continue along Divide Road for approximately 21.5 miles to Road #411 (Campbell Point Road). Turn right and travel west along Road #411 for 1.5 miles. Make a sharp left onto the Calcord Road and drive for about 0.5 mile. The road ends at the Calcord Cow Camp.

Trail Description: Head south along the fence line for 0.1 mile to a water trough. The trail continues south along the fence line at an easy grade. Hikers will pass through primarily aspen stands and oakbrush as the trail follows the contours along the hillside. After hiking approximately 7.5 miles, the trail intersects with the Long Canyon Trail. This is a good place either to turn back or to take the

Hiking in Roubideau Canyon

Long Canyon Trail back to your vehicle. This intersection is about 0.5 mile before the Weimer Cow Camp.

Alternative Route and Access: Hikers may also pick up the Upper Bench Tail from the Johnson Basin Road. Instead of turning right onto Road #411, continue traveling along Divide Road for 5 miles to Johnson Basin Road. A high-clearance vehicle is necessary to drive the Johnson Basin Road. Turn right (southwest) and drive for 1.5 miles, veering right at two forks to the Weimer Cow Camp. Park just outside the gate. Pick up the Long Canyon Trail (located about 50 feet before the gate). Hike north along a fence line (but don't go through the rustic gate), for approximately 0.5 mile; at this point, the trail intersects with the Upper Bench Trail. Both trails lead to Calcord Cow Camp.

Roubideau Canyon

Maps: USGS 7.5 minute map: Roubideau, Camel Back
Location: 55 miles from the Grand Junction Visitor Center
Elevation Range: 5,200—7,400 feet

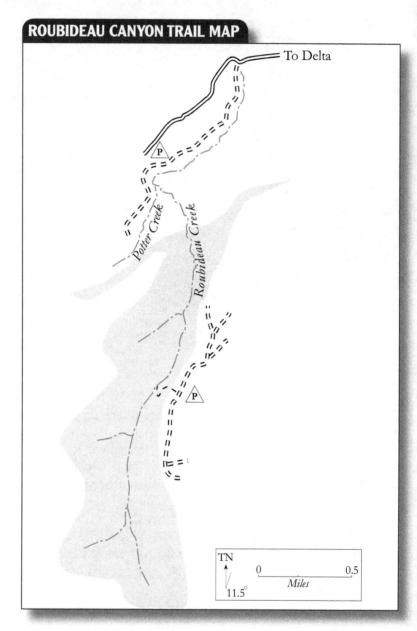

ROUBIDEAU CANYON TRAIL MAP

To Delta

P

Potter Creek

Roubideau Creek

P

TN
11.5°

0   0.5
Miles

Length of Hike (round trip): Varies; 2 miles to multi-day travel
Difficulty Rating: Easy
Seasons to Hike: All seasons
Special Features: Solitude; riparian ecosystem
Services: None

Managing Agency: Bureau of Land Management: Uncompahgre Basin Resource Area

Access: From the Visitor Center, turn left (south) onto Horizon Drive. At the roundabout, go straight. Turn left (south) onto 7th Street, then right onto Ute Avenue. Turn left (south) onto 5th Street, which eventually turns into Highway 50. Cross the 5th Street Bridge and drive southeast toward Delta on Highway 50. Continue for approximately 38.5 miles into the town of Delta. Turn right (west) onto 6th Street. This is the second turnoff for Highway 348. Look for the Public Lands Access—Uncompahgre Plateau sign. Continue following these signs, turning left (south) within 0.3 mile. Cross the Uncompahgre River and continue on Highway 348 as it climbs onto the mesa. When you reach a stop sign, turn right (west) onto D Road/Highway 348. Within 0.75 mile, continue straight, departing from Highway 348. This is Twenty-five Mesa Road. Within 3 miles, cross Roubideau Creek and turn left onto Lane 1100. A sign is posted for Roubideau Canyon. Follow this dirt road for 5 miles. Bear left at the fork and park before the creek crossing. This is the confluence of Potter Creek and Roubideau Creek.

Trail Description: Roubideau Creek is named after the French fur trapper Antoine Robideau. The lower reaches of this canyon consist of large groves of cottonwood trees growing along the perennial stream. The short canyon walls rise to sparsely covered desert terrain. Although there is no trail, the going is easy because hikers follow the stream up the canyon. Notice the cliff swallow nests along the cliff bands.

Wildcat Trail

Maps: U.S. Forest Service: Uncompahgre National Forest map; USGS 7.5 minute map: Snyder Flats
Location: 35 miles from the Grand Junction Visitor Center
Elevation Range: 7,000—7,800 feet
Length of Hike (round trip): Approximately 2 miles to the top of the canyon and back

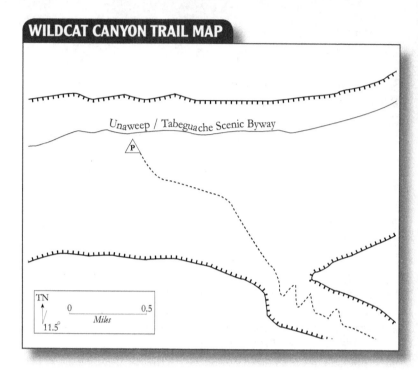

WILDCAT CANYON TRAIL MAP

Unaweep / Tabeguache Scenic Byway

TN
11.5°
0   Miles   0.5

Difficulty Rating: Moderate, except for very steep ascent up the
    side of the canyon
Seasons to Hike: Spring, summer, fall
Special Features: Scenic canyon views
Services: None
Managing Agency: U.S. Forest Service: Grand Valley Ranger District

Access: From the Visitor Center, turn left (south) onto Horizon
Drive. At the roundabout, go straight. Turn left (south) onto 7th
Street, then right onto Ute Avenue. Turn left (south) onto 5th
Street, which eventually turns into Highway 50. Cross the 5th
Street Bridge and drive southeast toward Delta on Highway 50.
Continue for approximately 8 miles to Whitewater. Travel 0.5 mile
to Highway 141 and turn right onto the Unaweep/Tabeguache
Scenic and Historic Byway. Take this beautiful route toward
Gateway. After approximately 13.5 miles, you will pass Divide
Road. Travel for 7 miles and park on the south side of the highway.
This spot is unmarked from the highway, but a barbed wire fence/
gate without a "No Trespassing" or "Private Property" sign marks
the location. You may pass through the barbed wire fence/gate

Hiking in Unaweep Canyon

with your vehicle, turn left immediately, and park next to a picnic table. Be sure to close the gate after you pass through.

Trail Description: Pass through a wooden gate and follow the forest service markers across the floor of the canyon in a southeast direction toward the canyon wall. When you reach a path/jeep trail running east/west, turn left (east) and follow the trail. Soon it begins its steep ascent through piñon pine, juniper, scrub oak, and sage. Continue along this old cattle trail up to the rim of the canyon, which is adorned by stands of aspen.

Unaweep Canyon Access Fund Trail

Maps: U.S. Forest Service: Uncompahgre National Forest map;
      USGS 7.5 minute map: Jacks Canyon
Location: 30 miles from the Grand Junction Visitor Center
Elevation Range: 6,800—8,000 feet
Length of Hike (round trip): 1 to 5 miles
Difficulty Rating: Moderate
Seasons to Hike: Spring, summer, fall, and dry winter days
Special Features: Sweeping views of Unaweep Canyon
Services: None
Managing Agency: The Access Fund

Access: From the Visitor Center, turn left (south) onto Horizon Drive. At the roundabout, go straight. Turn left (south) onto 7th Street, then right onto Ute Avenue. Turn left (south) onto 5th Street, which eventually turns into Highway 50. Cross the 5th Street Bridge and drive southeast toward Delta on Highway 50. Continue for approximately 8 miles to Whitewater. Travel 0.5 mile to Highway 141 and turn right onto the Unaweep/Tabeguache Scenic and Historic Byway. Take this beautiful route toward Gateway. After approximately 13.5 miles, you will pass Divide Road. Travel for 2.4 miles and park on the north side of the highway at a pullout with a walkover fence and two Access Fund signs.

Trail Description: This trail, located in the heart of Unaweep Canyon, would not exist without the efforts of the Access Fund. The Access Fund is a national, nonprofit climbers' organization that works to keep climbing areas open and conserve the climbing environment. The Access Fund purchased three prominent granite walls and a corridor across private property giving access

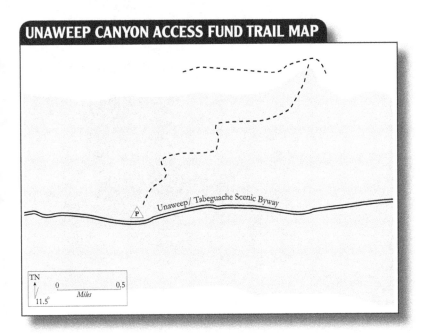

to these rock walls. In 1993, the Access Fund constructed the connecting trail system. Cross the walkover fence and follow the trail as it steadily climbs up to the base of the sheer granite cliffs and then swings right (east). You will probably see climbers enjoying this unique and pristine climbing area. Within about twenty minutes you will approach a fork. Go left as the trail follows along the base of the rock walls. The maintained section of the trail ends after another ten minutes of hiking. To continue, scramble up the rocky drainage. You will reach a terrace and the end of the drainage, which is marked by cairns, in approximately fifteen minutes. Continue left (west) on the rim by following the level trail. Hike for another mile or so and take in the stunning views of Unaweep Canyon from this vantage point.

Trail Notes

CHAPTER 9

Other Trails

These trails are scattered throughout the Grand Junction area
and do not specifically fall under one given heading.

BLM trails are primarily represented here.

Spanish Trail/Gunnison River Bluffs Area

Maps: BLM: Gunnison River Bluffs Trail/Spanish Trail
Location: 12 miles from the Grand Junction Visitor Center
Elevation Range: 4,700—4,700 feet
Length of Hike (round trip): 8 miles
Difficulty Rating: Easy
Seasons to Hike: All seasons
Special Features: Historic trail; scenic views
Services: None
Managing Agencies: Bureau of Land Management: the Grand
Junction Resource Area; the Mesa County Landfill
Management; the City of Grand Junction; the Grand
Junction/Mesa County Riverfront Commission; the
Orchard Mesa Irrigation District; the Museum of Western
Colorado; the Old Spanish Trail Association

Access: From the Visitor Center, turn left (southwest) onto Horizon
Drive. At the roundabout, continue traveling southwest. Turn left
(south) onto 7th Street, then right onto Ute Avenue. Turn left
(south) on 5th Street, which eventually turns into Highway 50.
Cross the 5th Street Bridge and drive southeast toward Delta on
Highway 50. Continue for approximately 5.7 miles to the Orchard
Mesa Landfill Road on the right and 30 3/4 Road on the left. Turn
right (west) toward the landfill and continue for about 0.5 mile.

SPANISH TRAIL MAP

P

Gunnison River

Old Spanish Trail

Gunnison Bluffs Trail

Hwy 50

Old Whitewater Road

P

TN

0   0.5

Miles

11.5°

Turn left immediately before the entrance to the landfill. Drive for another 1.5 miles to the trailhead and large parking area.

Trail Description: This 4-mile section of the Old Spanish Trail known as the Northern Branch of the Old Spanish Trail travels through the Gunnison River Bluffs Area. Following old Ute Indian trails, the Northern Branch was used by Spanish explorers in the early 1600s. In 1776, Spanish priests Dominguez and Escalante traveled this route in their expedition from Santa Fe to California. The trail was later used by trappers and traders in the 1800s. Today, this trail is open to hikers, equestrians, and mountain bike riders. In addition to the Spanish Trail, consider following the signs for the Gunnison River Bluffs Trail, which follows the rim of the Gunnison River. This scenic river is lined with lush riparian habitat that is a great contrast to the dry desert scrub along the Spanish Trail. The harsh ecosystem of Spanish Trail provides habitat for prairie dogs, lizards, and scorpions. Both trails are connected by several unmarked paths. Either trail will lead hikers to the northern trailhead; however, the Gunnison River Bluffs Trail is 2 miles longer than the Spanish Trail.

Alternative Access and Route: From the 5th Street Bridge, drive southeast toward Delta on Highway 50 as described above. Continue for approximately 3.3 miles. Turn right after the sign indicating "Fairgrounds Livestock Entrance." Take an immediate left turn (southeast). Within less than 0.1 of a mile, you will approach 28½ Road. Turn right on the dirt road that runs parallel to 28½ Road. This will lead to the northern trailhead. From the trailhead, follow a gravel road on foot and pass a small tree farm on the left. Follow signs for both the Spanish Trail and the Gunnison River Bluffs Trail System that briefly lead hikers through a neighborhood. Head north on Valley View Drive and then west on Sunlight Drive. A wide trail begins flanked by a split-rail fence.

Riggs Hill

Maps: Museum of Western Colorado: Riggs Hill trail map
Location: 9 miles from the Grand Junction Visitor Center
Elevation Range: 4,600—4,900 feet
Length of Hike (round trip): 0.75-mile loop trail
Difficulty Rating: Moderate
Seasons to Hike: All seasons
Special Features: Geology, quarry
Services: None
Managing Agencies: Bureau of Land Management: Grand Junction Resource Area; Museum of Western Colorado

Access: From the Visitor Center, turn left (southwest) onto Horizon Drive. At the roundabout, continue traveling southwest. Follow the signs for the Colorado National Monument by turning left (south) onto 7th Street, and then right (west) onto Grand Avenue. Pass through a major intersection with Highways 6 and 50 and cross the Colorado River. Grand Avenue is now Highway 340. Pass Monument Road and continue on Highway 340 for approximately 3 miles. Turn left onto South Broadway. Travel on this road for about 1 mile until you reach a parking area on the right side of the road.

Trail Description: This trail offers hikers a chance to visit a quarry area now called Riggs Hill. At the turn of the century, Elmer Riggs

RIGGS HILL TRAIL MAP

Riggs Hill

Broadway

P

South Broadway

TN
11.5°

0   Miles   0.5

inquired about fossil findings in rural western towns. Riggs was informed that local Grand Junction ranchers had been collecting bones since the area was opened to settlers in the early 1800s. In 1900, Riggs and his party spent the field season in the area and discovered the bones of a camarasaurus in what is now known as the Colorado National Monument. They continued exploring to the west and found the bones of a brachiosaurus. Several years later, local collectors discovered partial skeletons at Riggs Hill, which were left as part of a future natural exhibit. Unfortunately, the bones were removed by souvenir hunters before funds were raised for this site.

Dinosaur Hill

Maps: Museum of Western Colorado: Dinosaur Hill trail map
Location: 13 miles from the Grand Junction Visitor Center
Elevation Range: 4,600—4,800 feet
Length of Hike (round trip): 1-mile loop
Difficulty Rating: Moderate
Seasons to Hike: All seasons
Special Features: Geology
Services: Sheltered picnic area

DINOSAUR HILL TRAIL MAP

Dinosaur Hill

Highway 340

P

TN
▲
11.5°

0   0.5
Miles

Managing Agencies: Bureau of Land Management: Grand Junction Resource Area; Museum of Western Colorado; City of Fruita

Access: Travel west on I-70 towards Fruita for approximately 12 miles. Take Exit 19 (Highway 340) and turn left (south) at the stop sign. This is also the road to reach the west entrance of the Colorado National Monument. Follow the road for 1.6 miles, just past Kings View Estates. A parking area is located on the left (east) side of the road.

Trail Description: This loop trail offers hikers a chance to visit a quarry area now called Dinosaur Hill, which has ten points of interest. In 1901, Elmer Riggs, who was Assistant Curator of Paleontology at the Field Museum in Chicago, decided to dig in this area south of Fruita after spending the previous field season in the area now known as Riggs Hill. His crew built a boat to ferry supplies across the Colorado River. Riggs successfully excavated most of a brontosaurus.

Trail Notes

Bibliography

Chronic, Halka. *Roadside Geology of Colorado. Missoula*,
    Montana: Mountain Press Publishing Co., 1980.

Fagan, Damian. *Canyon Country Wildflowers*. Helena, Montana:
    Falcon Publishing Co., 1998.

Forgey, M.D., William. *Wilderness Medicine*. Merrillville, Indiana:
    ICS Books, Inc., 1994.

Johnson, David W. *Wildlife of the Canyons*. Fruita, Colorado:
    Colorado National Monument Association.

Kania, Alan J. *John Otto Trials and Trails*. Niwot, Colorado:
    University Press of Colorado, 1996.

Marsh, Charles S. *People of the Shining Mountains: The Utes of
    Colorado*. Boulder, Colorado: Pruett Publishing Co., 1982.

National Outdoor Leadership School. "Leave No Trace
    Principles." (March 15, 1999). Available: http:/www.LNT.org/
    LNTPrinciples/ LNT.principles.s&e.html

Pearson, Mark, and John Fielder. *Colorado's Canyon Country*.
    Englewood, Colorado: Westcliffe Publishers, Inc., 1995.

Rait, Mary. "Development of Grand Junction and the Colorado
    River Valley to Palisade from 1881 to 1931—Part I." *Journal
    of the Western Slope*, vol. 3. no. 3 (summer 1988).

———. "Development of Grand Junction and the Colorado River
    Valley to Palisade from 1881 to 1931—Part II." *Journal of
    the Western Slope*, vol. 3. no. 4 (autumn 1988).

Silbernagel, Bob. *Dinosaur Stalkers*. Fruita, Colorado:
    Dinamation International Society, 1996.

Smith, P. David. *Ouray: Chief of the Utes*. Ridgway, Colorado: Wayfinder Press, 1990.

Stall, Chris. *Animal Tracks of the Southwest*. Seattle, Washington: The Mountaineers, 1990.

Stokes, William Lee. *Scenes of the Plateau Lands and How They Came to Be*. Salt Lake City: Publishers Press, 1973.

Tilton, Buck. *Backcountry First Aid and Extended Care*. Merrillville, Indiana: ICS Books, Inc., 1994.

Index